DIRECT MAIL MARKETING
What works?
What doesn't work?
How to know the difference!

Joel N. Greene, Ph.D.

Direct Mail Marketing:
What Works? What Doesn't Work? How to Know the Difference!

Cover design by Luis C. Pangilinan

ISBN   - 978-1-7336319-0-7
Kindle- 978-1-7336319-1-4

I lovingly dedicate this book to
Lorna, Dara & Margaret
the three incredible women in my life
and to Ira
who has always been there
when I needed him
and to my grandchildren
Xavier, Gavin, Eoin, Harper, Scarlet & Alex

Table of Contents

LIST OF TABLES

8

LIST OF FIGURES

FOREWORD

Joel N. Greene, Ph.D. has written a remarkable book about direct mail marketing.

He offers a method using personalized direct mail to sell products and services that often generates response rates of 5% to 8% or more. Consider these numbers when marketing gurus generally concede that most direct mail efforts produce a meager 1% to 2% response rate, or lower.

This is a book that addresses the junk mail dilemma – our reliance on substandard forms of promotion that often annoy consumers and perform way below expectations. It defines what junk mail is and why it fails in the marketplace. Dr. Greene presents an abundance of examples of letters, post cards, and envelopes that demonstrate why his approach is so effective.

You will learn the solutions to many strategic direct marketing questions:

- Why an obsession with gaining attention often leads us astray?
- How demographics & psychographics fail as segmentation tools?
- Why power words like "free" often turn off prospective customers?
- How barcodes and postal indicia's lower response rates?
- Why direct snail mail can be more effective than digital marketing?

Dr. Greene's approach is nothing less than a paradigm shift for direct marketing. It is based on his 30 years of practical experience in the marketing trenches. As a director of Database Marketing, Dr. Greene managed 12 company websites and directed mailings to over 100 million consumers. His team was among the first to beta test the Postal Service's tracking systems for mass mailers.

Based on my years in the advertising agency industry, laboring over the creation of new promotions, one after the other – I can strongly recommend this concise book. Every page contains important methods or ideas that you can apply immediately to increase your own direct mail marketing acumen.

Go get them, and "thank you" Dr. Greene.

Howard I. Rothchild, M.Litt.
President/CEO
The Rothchild Group, Inc.

ABOUT THE AUTHOR

Joel N. Greene, Ph.D. is a direct marketing consultant. He was Director of Database Marketing at Sterling Jewelers Inc. (now Signet), the world's largest specialty retail jeweler. He managed all customer targeting and analytics for some 12 retail brands, and their websites, including Kay Jewelers and Jared. Dr. Greene was Vice President of ABS Direct, serving many Wall Street clients, including Citibank, Key Bank, Cyrus J. Lawrence, etc. Other clients have included AT&T, as well as the U.S. Departments of Commerce, Defense, and Energy. Dr. Greene has taught Marketing and International Business as a full-time faculty member at Hofstra University, Long Island University and Manhattan College. His doctorate in Marketing is from the Graduate Center, City University of New York. Dr. Greene initially worked in the financial industry as a Trust Officer with Bankers Trust Company, New York.

Please visit the author's Facebook page, *Directmailmarketing.*

ACKNOWLEDGMENTS

I want to thank the following individuals who have made this book possible:

John Estrella, a mentor and teacher, without whom, none of this would have happened. Thank you for making my dream come true and for sharing your knowledge and wisdom and experience.

Luis Pangilinan for using your wonderful graphic and artistic talents in designing the front and back covers. You have done an incredible job to make the book stand out.

Margaret Bradford for changing the title ever so slightly and perspicaciously!

Lorna Bonner, whose love, patience and literary guidance have been critical to this endeavor. Yes, there is always a woman behind it all!

Howard Rothschild, Harry Shapiro, and Rachelle Korland. Thank you for your friendship, expertise and help in bringing my minimus opus to a successful conclusion.

Chapter 1

Why Direct Mail Marketing?

Direct mail marketing is one of the most powerful and cost-effective promotional tools available, regardless of whether you manage a large corporation, non-profit, or sole proprietorship. It will provide you with a specific roadmap, enabling you to communicate with your existing or prospective clientele, about business-to-consumer or business-to-business products and services. Direct mail marketing promotes church services, new swimming pools, construction services, automobile repairs, legal and retail services, and many other types of products and services.

Direct mail marketing is in the marketing budgets of the majority of US companies today. The amount spent in the US on direct mail marketing annually is around $46 billion, which makes this medium the third largest expense following digital and TV advertising. Notably, it is close to the average combined media spending on radio, magazine, outdoor, and newspaper media.

When it comes to promoting your organization's products or services, it's easy to get distracted by today's technology. Who doesn't want to take advantage of online social media, such as Facebook or Amazon? Using emails, paid-for searches, and clickable offers represents a virtual world that is customizable, immediate, and segmentable. From this perspective, direct mail marketing or "snail" mail can look terribly obsolete and passé!

However, direct mail marketing provides the highest response rates of today's existing methods of promotions.

Figure 1. Estimated 2017 US Media Spending ($ Billions)
(Source: Statista.com)

Some Insights About Performance

Response rate is the best measure of promotional effectiveness or performance. It's relatively simple and shows the impact of a direct communication on the recipient. Did the recipient respond, either by returning a card, by calling an 800 number, by logging onto a website, or by clicking on a button to accept the offer? The Data & Marketing Association Statistical Fact Book (2017) indicates that the average response rates for different media are as follows: the average direct mail household response rate is 5.1%, compared to .6% for email, .6 % for paid search, .2% for online display, and .4% for social media. The DMA also found that direct mail response rates are ten to thirty times higher for direct mail than for digital media. (Data & Marketing Association, 2017).

Admittedly, it's important to note that an average response rate of 5.1% is quite high and that 1% may be closer to the average response rate achieved by most direct mail campaigns. A number of factors affect the rate, including the audience (existing clients or prospects), and whether the offer is free or involves some financial expenditure.

Nevertheless, the DMA statistics reflect an apparent advantage that email marketing has in comparison to direct mail marketing, as reflected by another statistic, return on investment (ROI). For direct mail, the average ROI appears to be about 29%, while the ROI for email campaigns averages almost 3 ½ times higher, or 124% (Data & Marketing Association, 2017). Which tells the true story, response rate or ROI?

Table 1 resolves this issue by showing sales results for the same product offered via these two channels using the average response and conversion rates for each form of media. Under identical conditions, direct mail marketing will produce significantly greater revenue and profit than email marketing.

Despite an ROI of 1.4% for direct mail vs. 8.3% for email (in Table 1), the direct mail campaign is 8x more profitable. Direct mail's higher conversion rate more than compensates for its lower ROI by generating revenue that is 12x higher than email.

In an article entitled, "Statistics That Prove Why Direct Mail Is Still King," Eric Laracuente recently extolled the advantages of direct mail marketing over its digital counterparts (Laracuente,2016). Steve Pulcinella, a marketer in the digital realm, also observed the continuing endurance and dominance of direct mail over time as a promotional medium (Pulcinella, 2017).

	Direct Mail	Email
Target Audience	10,000	10,000
Average Response Rate	.051%	.006%
Responses	510	60
Conversion rate	34%	24%
Product Price	$100	$100
Buyers	173	14
Revenue	$17,300	1,400
Cost	$7200	$150
Profit	$10,100	$1,250
ROI	1.4%	8.3%

Table 1 Direct Mail Vs. Email

Direct mail marketing has traditionally surpassed many other forms of media because of its superior ability to target its messages and to reach its intended recipients by name and location.   Digital media platforms (email, social media, etc.), however, have been narrowing this advantage, given their online tracking ability, individual customization of content, and real-time interactions with consumers.

Figure 2. shows the progressive amounts of targeting accuracy: from "Inaccurate" (for most forms of mass media promotions) to "Accurate" (for direct mail marketing, email and social media).

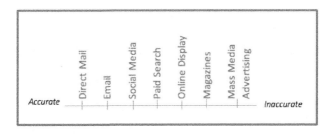

Figure 2. Targeting Accuracy

The relatively low response rates among digital media suggest that direct advertising in the cyber environment is much less effective in comparison to direct mail marketing. Email marketing, for example, literally inundates consumers with emails and spam. According to research conducted by marketingprofs.com, advertisers send out some 74 trillion emails each year, compared to 13.8 billion direct mail letters (Forer, 2017). Furthermore, the average lifespan of an email is only 2 seconds, while the average lifespan of a letter is about 17 days. Online consumers, therefore, have little time to process the information they receive. Moreover, the vast number of emails that the average person receives tends to over-load recipients (Forer, 2017).

Direct Mail's Distinctive Characteristics

Direct mail marketing appears to be better at creating a lasting or memorable impression among consumers. According to a MarketingProfs.com's 2017 survey, only 44% of people recalled a brand advertised online, compared to 75% of consumers who remembered receiving a brand promotion through direct mail (Forer, 2017). Presumably, people tend to remember items longer that engage their tactile senses, e.g., when they can feel or touch them.

The same survey reported that consumers also see the characteristics of direct mail and email quite differently, with direct mail having more lasting value. Consumers describe direct mail as "official, formal, important, believable, personal, and reliable." In contrast, the terms used by consumers to describe emails include "quick, spontaneous, smart, interesting and informal" (Forer, 2017).

Most marketers, in both the online or offline markets, try to establish long-term relationships with consumers, rather than generate one-time (e.g., non-repeating) sales. Marketers try to create sustainable, year-to-year revenue by increasing repeat business, customer loyalty, and patronage over time. The terms used to describe direct mail marketing tend to parallel these goals and suggest characteristics that are more substantial, long lasting and effective, while the email marketing comments appear to be more temporary, limited in scope, and situational. Although email is efficient and has advantages of speed and low cost, direct mail marketing commands greater consumer attention and impact.

SocialMediaWeek.org has also noted that direct mail marketing has embraced online technology, such as QR™ barcodes. Recipients simply scan the barcodes to visit general or personalized websites, where they obtain access to special online offers, etc. (Direct Mail Vs. Email, 2015).

Direct mail marketing also has a greater ability to convey a topic more fully, and in greater detail, than emails. A brochure provides the most complete explanation of a topic using text, photographs, multi-color charts and diagrams, and even cartoons or other illustrations. A well-written, multi-page brochure can educate the reader about complex topics, answer questions, and solve problems presumably faced by the reader. Consumers often read emails while commuting or during breaks, whereas they read brochures during their leisure hours, when they can focus greater attention on content (Direct Mail Vs. Email, 2015).

With ample room to convince and persuade the reader, the brochure itself can be a powerful sales tool. It can help overcome objections and minimize other concerns that prospective customers may have. For example, the brochure can help the reader to "get it," e.g., to fully grasp the personal benefits of choosing a particular brand or product.

Successful brochures provide reinforcement by highlighting perceived values and competitive advantages. If the brochure has accomplished its job, a consumer's apprehensions about prices and fees may also become less relevant. Without the brochure, the consumer often uses price to pre-judge the value of a commercial relationship or purchase. The lack of a brochure, or a poorly designed one, means that the customer can be easily lost to a cut-rate competitor.

The real backbone of the direct mail marketing industry are letters and postcards. Although there are no 140-character limitations in offline media, these tools must use text and illustrations judiciously and concisely. The letter and postcard are often the first promotional pieces that the recipient sees and/or reads. It is imperative that they contain only one message or theme, as well as well-chosen supporting benefits, that can convince the recipient either to reply or make a purchase.

The physicality of direct mail materials helps establish trust in the mind of the recipient. Typically, it demonstrates that someone has devoted some amount of time, funds and effort (e.g., printing, postage, etc.) to contact them on a one-on-one basis. In contrast, consumers may dismiss emails as unimportant and inconsequential. Since they lack substance, emails may experience greater difficulty in terms of engendering feelings of trust.

Direct mail marketing often involves the marketing of events, such as a special weekend sale. Invitations frequently offer discounts and rewards for past purchasing behavior (e.g., 30% off for best customers, 20% off for medium tier customers, and 10% off for new or lower spending customers). Advertising Age reports that 87% of all shoppers use coupons (Coupon Facts, 2017). Due to their short lifespans, coupons have the potential of creating excitement and urgency which increases both individual and total customer spending (Coupon Facts, 2017).

Periodic communications establish a relationship with customers that promotes and strengthens customer loyalty. Customers often wait for recurring sales, such as customer appreciation events that feature substantial discounts on selected merchandise. This can be particularly effective in retail settings, as a means of increasing store traffic, as well as for upselling and cross-selling.

How Direct Marketing Works

As Kurt Lewin has written, "there is nothing more practical than a good theory" (Lewin, 1952). Based on observations, a theory explains the relationships among variables that were not understood previously.

The most common model or theory of direct mail marketing and advertising is the popular AIDA model which stands for Attention, Interest, Desire, and Action. According to AIDA, the consumer must go through four stages before the promotion achieves success.

In the first stage, the promotion must be noticed and gain the customer's attention. Despite this objective, most direct mail winds up in the trash (and consumers delete the majority of emails they receive).

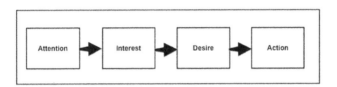

Figure 3. The AIDA Model

For many marketing practitioners, it is disturbing to realize that only 1% to 2% of an audience responds to a mailing, and that 98% to 99% of recipients discard promotional materials, unopened and unread.

Marketers often try to beat these odds by jazzing up the envelopes with headlines, different fonts, colors, and power words (such as free), and other call-outs. Advertisers believe that these items improve the chance of winning the recipients' attention.

The next challenge for the direct marketer is to create interest, stage two of the model. This is where you commonly find "irresistible" offers, including special event invitations, coupons, and "hero" photographs which present selected merchandise in the best light possible, imbued with images of love, elegance, sexiness, and group acceptance.

In the next stage, marketers employ two primary strategies to create desire. In the first, the promotional materials present "rational" offers which appeal to logical thinking and decision-making. Most likely, the promotional materials will display text and images about performance, cost-savings, value or investment worthiness, and endurance. Each of these addresses one's rational need.

Alternatively, the promotion focuses on "emotional" appeals that address the consumer's desires and wants. To tap Into these emotional reactions, the marketer will often use text and images associated with love, yearning, elegance, aspirations, style, sexiness, masculinity /femininity, attractiveness, and success.

Marketers sometimes believe that the product will sell itself, as shown in the first image below. While that is sometimes true, most consumers need to connect to their feelings and wants when it comes to their emotions. In Image 2, a couple in love uses emotion primarily (in lieu of the rational decision-making process).

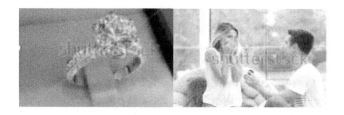

Figure 4. Rational vs. Emotional Appeals

In addition to emotional moments involving couples, family and friends, the tactile information that we receive through our senses also touches our emotional core. With the internet, what we see is not certain since so many online images are being photoshopped and altered. In real-life, we can get to experience tangible proof –- in the form of promotional materials and products – which makes us feel more secure and trusting.

With "Action," which is the final step in the AIDA equation, the consumer makes a purchase or responds to an offer. This means that two things have occurred: an inactive need of the consumer's is now fired up and activated, which leads in turn to the consumer feeling motivated to respond and make a purchase.

AIDA follows the classical stimulus-response model of human behavior, since the promotional materials represent a stimulus that causes or triggers the recipient to act in some way. Looking at direct mail marketing from the stimulus-response perspective can provide a strategic view of the overall buying process. While the following stimulus-response diagram is relatively simple, it may reveal additional opportunities for testing and using other variables

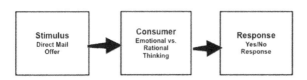

Figure 5. Stimulus-Response Model

(including different incentives, better pricing, or greater personalization) that could strengthen the impact of the stimulus to the consumer. The idea is to focus on the customer's journey and touchpoints from engagement through loyalty to make sure that the customer always experiences a high level of satisfaction.

Database Marketing

Organizations continue to use direct mail marketing as the engine to drive sales. In many organizations, the direct mail marketing group or department bears a more technical name, database marketing.

Database marketing primarily organizes and analyzes customer information (often collected at the store level), including customer name, location and buying history. Organizations can purchase and append a great deal of information to each customer record, such as demographics, media habits, marital status, car and boat ownership, education, and so on. The analysis of this information allows the organization to score each individual to focus its promotional efforts by targeting its best or most responsive customers.

Database architecture and software has progressed significantly over the years. Many organizations began their introduction to databases by recording customer information and addresses manually on index cards. Although index cards can provide a permanent record of the customer's personal information and purchases, they are not conducive to statistical analyses. In addition, manual systems are cumbersome, tend to lack standardization, and are subject to inaccuracies due to lost or misfiled cards.

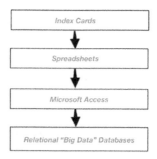

Figure 6. The Evolution of Databases:
From Spreadsheets to Relational "Big Data" Databases

The use of spreadsheets allows for creation of tabulated data tables and worksheets, storage, and formulas enhancing data calculations. However, most spreadsheets have data capacity limitations, such as one million rows of data per table. In addition, users must update spreadsheet data manually.

More complex programs, such as Microsoft Access, are relational database programs that have expanded the amount and integrity of the data stored as well as the types of analyses that marketers conduct on desktop computers. For example, users can create tables dedicated to specific raw data areas, such as customers, products, and purchases which can be queried for analysis, and updated instantly from various sources. Microsoft Access does have some limitations with respect to the number of simultaneous users, as well as data transfer methods.

Initially, mainframe computers hosted most consumer data so that in-house IT departments performed much of the programming and database maintenance activities. Responsibility for marketing databases has now shifted to the marketing department's own desktop computers which have computational capability to handle large databases as well as programming functions and statistical analysis. In many cases, the IT and marketing departments work jointly on many database issues.

Database marketing technology has truly come of age with the adoption of more sophisticated relational database programs such as Oracle, Teradata, SAP, and IBM. Each of these systems can handle unlimited amounts of data or "Big Data" analyses. These can be used for highly complex analyses of customer behavior, product promotions, and advertising performance.

The Customer Relationship Management (CRM) Approach

There are some alternatives to Database marketing technology. Many customer relationship management or CRM solutions are sales or salesforce oriented and use CRM software to track customer transactions and to plan promotions, including direct mail marketing and email campaigns. Organizations use CRM to provide a consistent understanding of the customer so that customer-based insights can be shared across different departments.

Built-in metrics provide a means for segmenting customer purchase histories or demographics to assist in the planning and implementation of mailed or digital promotional campaigns. CRM can also provide evaluations of different offers (known as A/B split tests) to determine which alternative creative or offer produced a higher response rate among different customer groups.

Response Rates and Online Channels

With more powerful computers and software, marketing departments can discover how to increase customer response rates in promotional campaigns. One solution for increasing response rates is to send promotions via multiple channels. Adding online media, such as email and social media campaigns, can produce a noticeable lift in response.

The growth of online communications as a way to engage consumers has been exponential. The Radicati Group, an online research company, points out that the number of worldwide internet users is now around 3.8 billion, exchanging some 280 billion emails daily. The number of email accounts, 6.3 billion, should also reach 7.71 billion by 2021 (Radicati Group, 2018).

Emails have become a ubiquitous part of life, and a common way for exchanging individual and business information and offers.

Direct mail marketers can use online social media channels as additional points of contact to complement direct mail campaigns. Social media too is growing and can provide an incredible array of opportunities to interact with existing and prospective customers. Statista (2018) indicates that roughly ¾ of all Americans have established profiles on social media websites. In the US, social media use will increase from 196 million people in 2016 to 216 million by 2021. In addition, the worldwide use of social media will increase from 2.34 billion people to 2.95 billion by 2020. Facebook alone has some 1.86 billion accounts, followed by YouTube and Whatsapp with 1.2 billion subscribers each (Statista, 2018).

Social media is a complex subject that means different things to different people. According to the online Merriam-Webster Dictionary, social media involves the creation of online communities that permit an exchange of information and personal viewpoints, images, and videos (Merriam-Webster Dictionary). Wikipedia suggests that social media are tools that enable the online exchange of information among individuals (Wikipedia.com).

To a large extent, these definitions describe how social media works, rather than what it is. From a marketing perspective, social media represent a revolution in the area of word-of-mouth communication among individuals as well as groups. In the past, word-of-mouth literally meant the spoken word conveyed verbally by one person to another. The meaning of word-of-mouth has changed and refers to interpersonal exchanges facilitated by online technology.

Marketers have long hoped to use word-of-mouth to create positive brand reactions. Reaching people directly online facilitates the ability to influence buyer choices and decisions. Social media also provides an ability to build contact lists and to reach, segment, and track groups of individuals in real time by customizing online offers, offering feedback, and providing relevant information.

Summary

This chapter covers a number of introductory topics about direct mail marketing. Many companies, particularly industry leaders, use direct mail marketing as the promotional engine driving growth and profitability.

Direct mail marketing produces the highest promotional response rates, provides a high level of precision, and possesses physical characteristics that are preferred by recipients, including Millennials who have grown up with the internet and with digital advertising (Pulcinella, 2017). Direct mail marketing is a powerful form of promotion that offers an ability to identify and reach key recipients in the market.

Email and social media complement direct mail marketing efforts. In addition to building our lists of online subscribers and prospects from our existing clientele, we can create compelling online activities that attract new subscribers who opt in to our websites, blogs, podcasts, and social media groups. We can also use list brokers who can provide prospect lists to match the key psychographic, demographic and behavioral characteristics of our best customers.

Like most things in life, direct mail marketing adheres, in part, to the laws of probability. At any given time, there are potential customers in your marketplace who want to buy your products or services. These customers will respond positively if your mailing or online efforts are well timed. In a subsequent time-frame, a different group of consumers will react to another wave of mailings.

This process follows an old axiom in golf that advises, "the more you practice, the luckier you get." The same is true in consumer promotions. Direct mail marketing efforts improve with use.

Action Steps

Pick any direct mail piece in your mailbox that you have recently received. Examine the contents and see if they offer you an online destination to continue a relationship with you. Do they tell you to go to their general dot.com website, or have they created a special landing page on their website that continues the offer or conversation they started via direct mail? Is it a seamless transition or do you have to search again for the product or service you are interested in?

In addition, how well coordinated would you say the sender's efforts are offline and online? Are prices the same online and offline? Are all the same products and brands available online and offline?

Chapter 2

The 12 Deadly Sins of Direct Marketing

How would you feel about receiving the following item in your mailbox?

Figure 7. An Attention Getter?

Yes, it's a red brick, weighing approximately 7.7 pounds! The sender is a large Direct Mail Agency in New York. A letter accompanying the brick explains that "we planned to throw the brick through your window to gain your attention, but we decided to mail it instead."

Undoubtedly, its unique contents would capture your attention. Presumably, the Agency figured that this unique mailing would also provide proof of their superior creative ability. The question is: "would you hire them?"

Hopefully, you realize that mailing a brick is not suitable for a direct mail campaign. Consider the cost of postage alone, around $8 per package for regular mail, and $18 for priority mail. The initial idea of throwing it through your window is at best silly, and at worst dangerous.

Instead of demonstrating how the Agency would help you communicate to your clientele more effectively, the Agency has resorted to using a "gimmick," which is, in actuality, a cheap trick or stunt. It is doubtless one of the worst direct mail marketing examples you will ever see. The mailing offers little insight into the Agency's ability to communicate convincingly. Even if you are selling bricks, it fails miserably!

The "brick" example also demonstrates the direct mail industry's obsession with gaining attention at almost any cost. What this attention gaining preoccupation leads to is an over-reliance on methods that many marketers think "creates excitement" or "stands out from the crowd and the clutter." Attention getting methods include the use of "buzzwords" and "power words," such as "free," "exclusive," "sale," and the use of "bright colors and images." It also includes "snappy headlines" on the outside of the envelopes and postcards that companies send to targeted recipients.

When promotional pieces reflect the use of gimmicks, power words, and other garish techniques, the resulting pieces tend to be what we think of as *Junk Mail.* Let's get a better understanding of what junk mail is by considering the following definitions:

- The Merriam-Webster Dictionary defines junk mail in terms of quantity, as "advertisements, solicitations, etc. *mailed in large quantities*, usually by third class mail" (Merriam-Webster Dictionary).

- The online Business Dictionary recognizes junk mail as a social burden and comes closer to the mark in defining junk mail as *"unsolicited mail"* (Businessdictionary.com).

- The Collins Dictionary comes even closer to the heart of the matter, in defining junk mail as "advertisements and publicity materials in your mail that *you have not asked for and that you do not want"* (Collinsdictionary.com).

Typically, junk mail includes a cluster of specific characteristics that the consumer views as negative, insincere, and even garish. We call these characteristics the "12 Deadly Sins of Direct Marketing," as shown in Figure 8.

- *Unconcerned with the User's Welfare*
- *Impersonal*
- *Focuses on Product Features*
- *Looks Mass Produced*
- *Is self-Aggrandizing*
- *Gimmicky*
- *Cluttered*
- *Deceptive*
- *Devoid of Benefits*
- *Lacks One Unifying Theme*
- *Send Money Oriented*
- *Expensive but looks Cheap*

Figure 8. The 12 Deadly Sins of Direct Marketing

Notably, if a recipient perceives just one of these characteristics, it would be sufficient to classify the piece as junk mail. When a cluster of the "12 Deadly Sins of Direct Marketing" characteristics is perceived, there is no doubt about its junk mail classification.

Junk Mail Envelopes

Perhaps our biggest clue about junk mail concerns the visual design of the envelope that first appears in our mailbox. For example, envelopes sometimes mimic the look of official government pieces (which most people would presumably open immediately).

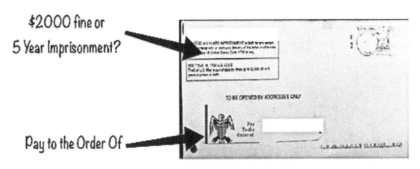

Figure 9. Faux Govt. Envelope

Our initial envelope example appears to be an official government envelope. An official warning of $2000 in fines is threatened for obstructing its delivery per the US Code, while the second box adds a threat of jail time for theft of US property.

The idea is that the recipient will feel compelled to open an official piece of US Mail. The look-alike envelope has no relationship to the government at all. Instead, the envelope contains marketing materials and a product or service offer.

With "Pay to the Order Of" displayed on the envelope itself, or through the envelope window, the recipient is enticed to believe they have received an unexpected windfall.

Of course, the "check" inside is a non-negotiable coupon that offers a discount if the recipient makes a purchase.

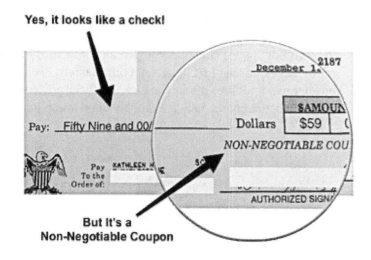

Figure 10. The Non-Negotiable Coupon

The following example is an envelope that comes from a non-profit organization. You can tell who the source is (without opening the envelope) because it bears an indicia or metered postage that says, "NONPROFIT U.S. POSTAGE."

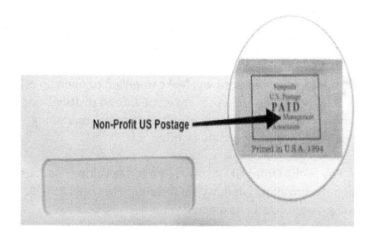

Figure 11. Non-Profit Indicia

The non-profit sector undoubtedly feels that its mailings gain the recipient's trust and attention by carrying this identifiable postage imprint. And, as long as the automated mailings bear a non-profit stamp or pre-paid indicia, the non-profit organization receives a U.S. postal discount.

How do recipients respond to this postage? Oftentimes, the reaction is to throw the envelope and its content in the trash, since one can assume that the materials inside are only seeking a donation. To counter this trend, many non-profits enclose free address labels to encourage contributions. Of course, the mailings are discarded, but the labels are used.

An interesting question exists for non-profit organizations that experience low response rates: if the non-profit sender forgoes the postal discount by using "first-class" postage, would opening and response increase? Would the rate of donations also increase? You can be certain that both the responses and donations would increase! Can you explain why?

The following envelope's characteristics also give the recipient some clues as to whether or not the envelope should be opened. Although personally addressed, the envelope also bears a pre-sorted, standard postage indicium, and an automated barcode, indicative of a large mass-mailing.

All of these characteristics affect response rate. Without even considering the content of the following envelope, factors such as an automated barcode and pre-sorted, metered indicia contribute to an impersonal appearance that causes low response rates.

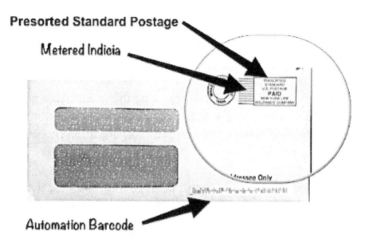

Figure 12. Pre-sorted Indicia

What overall impression does the above envelope make? Would you open it or discard it without reading the contents?

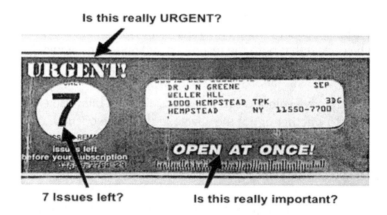

Figure 13. "Urgent" Call-out Messages

The envelope shown above contains three "call-out" messages: it declares that the contents are "URGENT!" in capital letters and exclamation point! Next, it orders the recipient to "OPEN AT ONCE!" again in capitals with an exclamatory emphasis. The number 7 in the circle warns the recipient that there are only "7 issues left." Presumably, this mailing contains a notice that a magazine subscription is about to expire and that a renewal is urgently needed to avoid any disruption in service.

What makes this envelope fall into the category of "junk mail"? For one thing, it feels "mass-produced." This is not an envelope that a friend or relative would send you. Although it may be addressed to you, the graphic design and execution of copy are impersonal.

Messages and dire warnings clutter the envelope without offering any real benefits. Knowing that one's magazine subscription is ending is important, but the expiration apparently won't happen for another 7 issues, perhaps in seven months, a time-frame that doesn't seem urgent.

All of these envelopes represent examples of what we normally think of as "junk mail." In general, the envelopes contain elements that evoke feelings of impersonalization and mass production.

Although these materials may be expensive to create and mail, their response rates are typically poor due to the recipient's ability to recognize the envelope as containing "junk mail." For the consumer, there may be little risk associated with discarding the entire mailing without examining its contents.

Human beings employ a process of selective perception, which focuses their attention on items of interest that meet expectations. The consumer ignores all other items that fail to meet this perceptual threshold. If the marketer is successful, he has caught the consumer's attention, ensuring further consideration of his product or service.

The primary objective of the envelopes shown here is to gain attention by breaking through mailbox clutter and noise. In fact, the direct mail industry is obsessed with the creation of awareness by almost any means to gain the recipients' attention.

The recipient's level of awareness and emotional response can range from positive to negative to indifferent. Obviously, the best result is a positive one, with the promotional materials evoking a positive response towards the product or service as well as towards the company or sender. The mailing itself may provide positive reinforcement to an already agreeable attitude, which helps in the overall formation of customer loyalty.

However, the mailing may also provoke a negative response, possibly due to a previously adverse experience with the company or its products. Each time the consumer discards or ignores the mail piece, the promotional impact or effectiveness diminishes. Repeated negative responses mean that the likelihood of doing business with a particular individual has been virtually extinguished.

Interestingly, if the recipient chooses to provide feedback by voicing their objection about receiving the promotion (often to store personnel or more formally to Customer Relations), the feedback could create an opportunity to intervene and counter the customer's objections or negative attitudes, and possibly rekindle a more positive view for the future.

An indifferent response may mean that there is little demand for the offering, or else the marketer hasn't tapped into the market's needs very well, nor articulated any meaningful benefits. The recipient essentially views the product or service neutrally or as having minimal value. The recipient may simply ignore the promotional offer if they are already satisfied with a competitor's product or service.

Marketers can easily over-do their creative efforts to gain attention. For example, the next envelope undoubtedly seeks to break out of the mold of boring mail and cluttered mailboxes. It reflects a misplaced sense of humor in that it resembles a blackmail or ransom note.

Figure 14. A "Ransom" Envelope

Junk Mail Letters

Its accompanying letter, in Figure 15, also exhibits a similar message. Unfortunately, this is just another "gimmick" designed to gain attention. It too provides little reason for a positive reply. The ransom note gimmick is largely unrelated to the offer itself, and it does little to enhance the reasons or benefits for purchase.

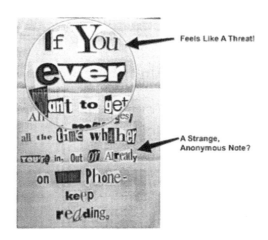

Figure 15. A "Ransom" Letter

Promotional letters rarely "travel" alone. Instead, the envelope is stuffed with other items, including "lift letters" that tend to look like greeting cards, as well as coupons, address labels, pens, surveys, and order forms.

Most direct mail letters bear little resemblance to the usual letter you might receive from a friend or relative. Instead, they most likely employ a mixture of headlines and texts of different colors, exclamation points, and emphases by use of different fonts, underlining and bold highlights.

Marketers also place considerable faith in the use of power words. As shown in Figure 16, we see part of a letter where the word, FREE, appears to be the most important element in the entire promotion:

Figure 16. The Power of "FREE"

Indeed, offering something for "FREE" is one of many seductive techniques in the marketing wordsmith's toolshed or "spiders web." These techniques employ hundreds of potent words and expressions to ensnare the less vigilant recipient with prizes, discounts, trial offers, and invitations. All of these enticements promise "complete satisfaction."

FREE is a powerful motivator. Marketers use such words to sell because they have been proven effective in the past. Yet, it is not a panacea for poorly written direct mail promotional materials that lack focus or are devoid of benefits.

Some marketers use leading questions to elicit a "yes" response, or subconscious agreement with an offer, which makes the customer feel acquiescent and raises the likelihood of their making an unintended purchase. Alternatively, the promotion may entail an impending deadline, requiring an immediate decision, since the offer is only good for a limited time. These are heavy handed techniques that trick the consumer into buying compulsively.

Unfortunately, an over-reliance on power words and other manipulative techniques will inevitably harm the direct mail industry in the long run. People do not like to question their purchases after the fact, but the use of verbal or written manipulation often leads to post-purchase dissonance and buyer remorse. Direct marketing communications should present products and services in a clear manner that is easily understood, without resorting to questionable words and/or psychological practices that are almost subliminal in nature.

Communication problems may also be caused inadvertently by poorly written promotions. Ironically, direct marketers frequently don't know how to compose a concise, persuasive letter that clearly presents the key benefits to the consumer. The result is a letter that often rambles along without a clear focus or objective. Oftentimes, the letter simply lacks any real benefits or useful information.

The next letter is marred by an impersonal greeting as well as a headline which is more appropriate for advertising than for a personal letter. Although the letter lists a number of facts or characteristics about the service being offered, none of the benefits are clearly spelled out.

Figure 17. Lack of Benefits

Figure 18 shows part of a three-page letter offering recipients a chance to buy a publication to help them win government financial grants.

Unfortunately, the most important benefits are buried on the bottom of the second page of the letter. Few recipients, if any, would spend the necessary time looking through all of the unnecessary verbiage in the entire letter to see where the "gold" resides.

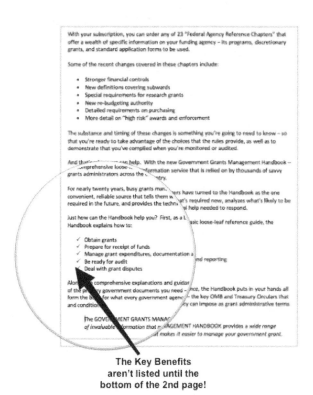

**The Key Benefits
aren't listed until the
bottom of the 2nd page!**

Figure 18. Hard to Find Benefits

The writer should have highlighted the key benefits on page one!
Instead, they are buried deep in the text. Finding them is a tedious
and onerous task. It is the writer's duty to highlight how the offer
satisfies the consumer's needs.

The bulk of the letter above describes the characteristics of the
offer without providing any explanation of how they benefit the
recipient. Writers often expect the readers to understand how the
offer's characteristics intuitively meet their needs. That rarely
happens. Instead, it is up to the writer to explain how each element
of the offer will improve the life of the recipient.

The following letter again offers something FREE – this time, a FREE workshop that the recipient is invited to attend to learn about a new career opportunity. The writer spends most of the time praising himself without offering details about the program. This is self-aggrandizement, which extols the virtues of the writer or company ("established in 1903;" "#1 in its industry"), while ignoring the needs and wants of the recipients.

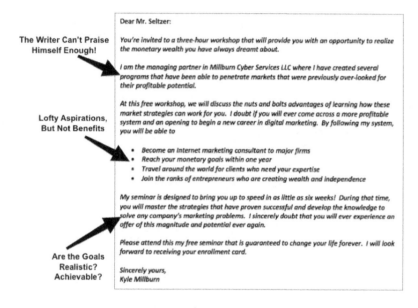

Figure 19. A Self-Aggrandizing Letter

The thrust of the promotion should be about the recipient. What specific needs does the recipient have and what are realistic chances for successful improvement? Since an instructional seminar is being offered, the letter should spell out the specific skills and techniques that are being taught. Unfortunately, the letter appears to be intentionally secretive or vague about the services being presented. The letter should openly provide details about the program's content and approach, and it should cite examples of individuals who have achieved their goals because of the system.

A truthful approach provides consumers a concrete basis for evaluating the promotion and whether it merits further consideration. From an ethical perspective, long-term promotional truthfulness, rather than puffery and self-adulation, is infinitely more effective and profitable!

The next direct marketing letter seeks to attract new members to an academic organization. The letter, which has been sent to educators, starts off with a controversial quote about teaching and students. Essentially, the quote is a gimmick to gain attention, and while it does stand out, it unfortunately disparages the teaching profession. Thus, it gains attention for the wrong reasons, and presumably offends its intended recipients!

> "Teaching, I find, is not the most amusing thing on earth; in fact, with a stupid lump for a Pupil, it is about the most irksome."
> Jane Welsch Carlyle, Scottish Writer (1801-1866)

Dr. Brad Britain
Department of Marketing
Hofstra University
Zarb School of Business
Hempstead, NY 11550

Dear Brad:

There are a lot of academic associations which help to support the academic profession. The National Alliance of Marketing Academics (NAMA) focuses on all teaching and classroom skills as they relate to marketing. NAMA is the one place to go where you can discover cutting edge techniques, be introduced to new technologies, and find unique 21st century marketing topics.

There are many reasons why you should consider joining NAMA:

- Exceptionally Low Membership Dues – Our members are the managers and worker bees! We think the low annual dues of $250 is a bargain compared to other groups.
- We are marketing educators with an interest in pedagogical topics. You won't find a better place to learn new and stimulating presentation and teaching skills!

The enclosed multi-page brochure contains a complete list of topics being presented at our upcoming conventions. Our next convention, on January 15-18, 2019, will cover New Methods of International Marketing Instruction, and will be held at the Atlanta Hyatt Regency Hotel. Please make your reservation before January 10th to receive a 15% discount.

I am looking forward to welcoming you to NAMA and to meeting you in person,

Very truly yours,

Dr. Jayson North

Figure 20. The "Shot-Gun" Approach

The writer makes additional mistakes. The letter contains a "laundry list" of reasons for becoming a member, including the low amount of dues, opportunities to learn about advances in pedagogy, and invitations to attend semi-annual conventions. This is a shot-gun approach.

The writer apparently hopes that one of the reasons cited in the letter turns out to be meaningful to the reader. It misses the mark since it fails to focus on benefits, e.g., how becoming a member of the organization will improve the reader's career or personal life. The letter would be considerably more effective as a promotional tool had the writer used a single theme or message.

For example, the writer mentions "presentation skills" among the pedagogical approaches. The letter could easily focus on this one subject. How would membership in this organization improve my presentation skills and make me a better presenter and teacher? The organization's letter in this example could then discuss some presentation skills that new members might desire, such as:

- The importance of topic clarity and focus

- Tailoring your presentation to your audience

- Why each visual contains only one main subject

- How to declutter visuals by omitting chatter

- Matching statistics to context, etc.

The writer must show how the chosen promotional topic fulfills the skill development needs and interests of the recipients.

The importance of choosing one message or theme for the promotional letter cannot be overemphasized. A single topic letter is easier to understand by the reader, and this will result in higher response rates compared to letters that fail to focus on one particular issue or message,

Summary

The examples in this chapter contain characteristics, including what we call the "12 Deadly Sins of Direct Marketing," that lower response rates. They typify promotions that we usually label as *Junk Mail*, which seem to include the majority of promotional mail we receive each day.

Recall that companies send junk mail to large groups of individuals simultaneously. The promotional materials carry the signs of automation and mass mailings, e.g., metered postage or a prepaid or pre-sorted indicia and barcodes.

Although many examples of mass-produced mail are unsolicited and unwanted, it is true that there are desirable items among the clutter. For example, recipients sometimes eagerly anticipate and desire the arrival of store coupons and sales event invitations.

Although enclosed coupons and price discounts may help in the consumer's decision process, care must be taken since non-price benefits tend to be more effective and longer lasting. It's important to know how to create mass produced materials that have value and are not jettisoned as junk mail.

A better way to strengthen direct mail communication is for marketers to improve the design and appearance of the promotional materials. The key is to transform "junk mail" into something that appears to be more desirable, that will be read, and that will lead to positive action. The next chapter will discuss this more fully.

Action Steps

When your mail arrives at home or at your office, see if you can spot a "junk" mail item. What makes it stand out as being junk mail? Open the envelope and examine the contents.

How many of the mail items use gimmicks to gain your attention? How many gimmicks can you spot?

Having read this chapter, what do you think about the mail that you found? Do the promotional pieces leave you with a positive, negative or indifferent feeling? Why is that?

CHAPTER 3

USING PERSONALIZED DIRECT MAIL

What makes a direct mail campaign effective? It begins with the letter.

An effective direct marketing letter doesn't feel or look like junk mail. There are no graphics, no buzz words or power expressions, and no lofty claims about the product, service, company or writer. Although this may sound like direct marketing heresy, the best direct marketing letter is simply, a letter. Its purpose is to communicate an offer or information in as direct and candid a manner as possible. An accompanying direct marketing envelope should also be a plain, unadorned envelope that uses a real first-class stamp (versus the typical pre-sorted, postage metered indicia). Together, the direct marketing letter and envelope resemble an ordinary message sent by one individual to another.

As far as response rates, it is the personal nature, tone, and appearance of the promotion that determines whether it is read or not. The glitziness of a junk mail piece is an unnecessary distraction that impedes communication. Despite the use of power words, headlines, and other attention-grabbing devices, the benefits of the offer often go unstated or unnoticed, so that the recipient never really comprehends the reasons for buying.

In this chapter, we will first look at various direct mail letters that performed well. They are effective because each letter focuses on the needs and desires of their audiences.

Personalized Direct Mail Letters

In Figure 21, we start with a very simple letter for a small real estate agency that was written almost 30 years ago. It still appears to have vitality and relevance to the marketplace today as the day it was written.

Dear Roger,

As a landlord, what are you most concerned about ---getting maximum rents from reliable tenants and minimizing costs.

In these times, we realize it is difficult to find the right solutions and the people who can appreciate your problems. Seeking good tenants and helping you is <u>our business.</u>

My name is <u>Anthony James</u> ---

You have dealt with me over the years as Vice-President of Forest Realty. In order to serve you better, I have now formed <u>Tru House Realty</u> --- where you can get professional service by full-time realty specialists.

We look forward to being of service to you at our <u>TruHouse!</u>

Yours truly,
Anthony James

Figure 21. Real Estate Agency Letter

The first sentence of the letter addresses the recipient and his primary problems and offers a solution in terms of the writer's business. The writer introduces his history with the recipient as the foundation of the new relationship being offered. He provides some additional details concerning his qualifications and reiterates the professional benefits that are being offered.

The writer does not suggest any actions that the recipient should take, and that is probably the letter's one flaw. The writer could have indicated that he intended to call or visit the recipient next week. In addition, the writer can offer something that the recipient would need to request, such as a brochure. Alternatively, the letter could instruct the recipient to download a pdf file or else direct the reader to a customized website landing page. Getting the recipient to do something active helps advance the relationship to the next level, (in this case, a contract or assignment) which helps to cement the new business connection.

The next letter provides another business-to-business (B2B) example that demonstrates how a direct mail letter can use a personalized direct mail format that is simple and persuasive.

Dear Daniel,

Experience has shown that Personalized Direct Mail is the single, most cost-effective method for obtaining new customers, as well as immediate and long-term sales. As a business manager, you appreciate how a Personalized Direct Mail campaign can help ensure your business' continued growth and prosperity. For example, with a Personalized Direct Mail campaign, you will be able to

- Establish a quality image for your products and services;
- Produce long-term relationships and loyal customers for your firm;
- Reach only your most likely purchasers, thereby minimizing unproductive personal selling time and/or media coverage;
- Add immediate sales and profits to your bottom line.

At Dara Associates, we have been creating Personalized Direct Mail campaigns for over 20 years. Based on your firm's unique capabilities, as well as the needs of your market, we will develop a persuasive theme which acts as the focal point of your campaign. Our promotional materials effectively communicate your company's distinctive benefits, thereby achieving the desired impact and results.

If you would like to receive more information about how our customized Personal Mail Campaign can help you gain new customers and sales, please return the enclosed response letter or call me. I look forward to hearing from you soon,

Sincerely

Figure 22. Direct Mail Services Letter

The letter is very straight forward and starts by identifying the subject area – personalized direct mail services– along with two primary benefits. Most importantly, the letter looks at the service offering from the recipient's point of view – and the dual benefits that the recipient desires, e.g., business growth and prosperity.

The benefits of personalized direct mail are now explained in a succinct bulleted list. These benefits are followed by a paragraph describing additional details about the writer's services, emphasizing once again how he can help the recipient achieve the "desired impact, high response rates, and maximum sales results." The last paragraph of the letter focuses again on benefits and reiterates the sales results that can be achieved.

Finally, the letter suggests two ways that the recipient can respond to the letter. it's good practice in the body of the letter to suggest how the recipient should respond.

The common response mechanisms include post cards, 800 telephone numbers, and barcodes (which lead to customized webpages).

The response mechanism recommended here is a Response Letter. This letter is pre-addressed to the original sender and is accompanied by a small envelope that is also pre-stamped to facilitate its return.

We use a response letter for the same reason that we prefer to mail our promotional campaigns via first class mail. A stamped envelope makes the mailing appear personal and individualized.

Mr. Bill Thompson
Dara Associates
254 West 54th Street
New York, New York 10019

Dear Mr. Thompson,

I am interested in finding out how Personalized Direct Marketing can help my company obtain new sales and profits.

☐ Please call me at Tel #_____

☐ Please call my associate_____
        Tel #_____

☐ Please send me a copy of your new brochure, "How To Find New Customers"

☐ I may be interested in the future. Please keep my name on your active mailing list.
Sincerely,
Daniel Williams

Figure 23. Response Letter Format

Most of the promotional letters in this chapter use a general template, shown in Fig. 24. These letters work well. Nevertheless, please feel free to experiment and make changes that you deem appropriate for your market.

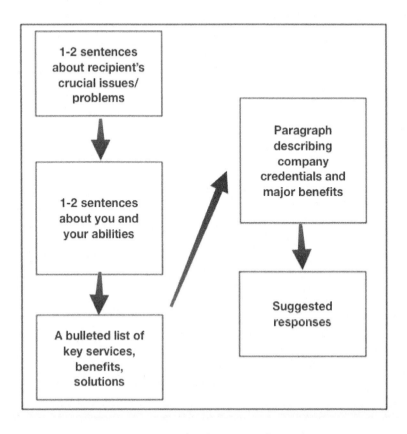

Figure 24. Personalized Direct Mail Template

The next direct marketing example was developed to market new swimming pools to homeowners. In this situation, the direct marketing firm had to determine the best way to find and target potential in-ground swimming pool buyers. The solution used here involved compiling a list of neighbors within the proximity of homes where a pool had just been installed. Sometimes, the best lists can be found using common sense, rather than buying them from list brokers or agencies.

The letter introduces its purpose in the first two sentences. The bulleted list of benefits focuses on the lifestyle advantages that the recipient stands to gain. Each benefit completes the lead-in sentence from the previous paragraph and shows how the product will improve the home and the owner's lifestyle. Some of the words are capitalized so that they "jump out" at the reader. It's a minor embellishment, but it helps to drive home the message without distracting the reader from the overall message.

Dear Mr. Andrews,

The enclosed photograph shows a new in-ground swimming pool which Sun Fun Systems recently installed for one of your neighbors.

We understand that you might be interested in the benefits of a similar addition to your home. If you've ever considered an in-ground pool before, you know that it adds

- Elegant and Gracious Living space to your home
- Complete Relaxation, Better Health, and Enjoyment in your own pool
- An Elegant Setting for Socializing and Entertaining Your Friends, Business Associates, and Neighbors
- A Garden Atmosphere of Serenity, Beauty, and Comfort

You can even begin to enjoy the pleasures of your own pool before the end of this Summer. Indeed, we are the only in-ground specialists in Ohio who personally install what we sell. In addition, we provide the longest customer warrantees of any of Ohio's pool firms.

We would be delighted to help you in planning or designing a swimming pool which will suit your home and lifestyle. For more information, please return the enclosed, stamped return envelope and we will send you a new brochure describing your pool in more detail. There is no obligation.

Sincerely,
Trevor Addams

Figure 25. Residential Pool Letter

The next to last paragraph suggests a deadline if the recipient wants to have the installation completed before the end of the summer. The balance of the paragraph describes the advantages of dealing with this particular vendor or company.

The inclusion of a photograph, shown in Fig 26, of the latest pool installation follows the old adage of the "product selling itself." The idea of using a photograph, drawing or other visual is simple and effective. It grounds the reader and realistically demonstrates the beauty or utility that the product or service offers.

Figure 26. Photograph Insert

The letter offers the recipient an opportunity to request a brochure. At the same time, they are reassured that such a request involves no obligation or commitment on their part. By requesting the brochure, the recipient self-selects from being a prospect to that of a more likely buyer. Once the brochure has been sent, a follow-up call will help close the deal. The telephone call allows the marketer to confirm that the consumer received the brochure. It also provides an opportunity to answer any additional questions that the person may have, as well as set a time and date to get together in order to examine the property and plan where the pool would be located. These steps will be discussed later in the telemarketing section of this chapter.

The next letter begins with a question: "Did you know that there is a remarkable school located right here in Northern Ohio?" This question is adaptable to a host of situations and is an effective opening that immediately engages the reader.

Dear Mrs. Johnson,

Did you know that there is a remarkable school for your children located right here in Northeast Ohio where each child learns how to lead a life of leadership and accomplishment? Graduates of Waldorf schools around the world often attribute their education as the foundation which enabled them to succeed as top executives, educators, lawyers, physicians, and government leaders, among others.

Spring Garden Waldorf School follows educational principles that focus on nurturing and developing the individual skills, talents, and self-esteem of each student through learning by actual hands on experience, so that every student is prepared to excel in life. We do this by:

- Creating a supportive and motivating educational experience for children from preschool through eighth grade in which each child's learning needs are met without overemphasis on testing and competition
- Using music, foreign language, and the arts to help develop individual proficiencies
- Working with the same class teacher from first through eighth grade so that the educational experience reflects continuity and re-assurance
- Developing a healthy "can do" attitude by engaging the child in cooperative and challenging nature activities that create a sense of accomplishment and confidence

In short, Spring Garden Waldorf's School's curriculum and approach is unique in that it seeks to educate the whole human being so that the child develops into a confident thinker and a skilled and successful doer.

You are invited to find out more about Spring Garden Waldorf School and how this wonderful educational experience can benefit your child. You will find that Spring Garden is a very affordable alternative to other private schools and to the public school system.

For your convenience, I've enclosed a pre-paid return postcard for your use to learn more about our school and upcoming open house events. In addition, please call or email me directly to ack any question or to schedule a personal visit for you and your child to see our school in person.

Sincerely,

M. Sullivan
Admissions Director

Figure 27. "Did you know?" Letter

The letter reiterates many specific benefits, followed by a suggestion that the recipient return the "prepaid postcard" and consider scheduling a visit to the school. The promotion produced a substantial number of replies and visits by parents.

The following letter was sent to attorneys in Northeast Ohio by Decision Point Research, a firm that uses mock trials to aid in juror selection and courtroom strategy. After bulleting several benefits, the letter advances a tag line, "a mock trial is your best defense," which resonates strongly with its intended audience.

The list of recipients for this campaign was assembled by using several sources, including Martindale Hubbell, which lists law firms by location and specialization (e. g., trial attorneys.). In addition, social media sites, such as LinkedIn and Facebook, are excellent sources for mail and email lists of qualified recipients.

Dear Mr. Smith:

Did you know that there is an experienced mock jury trial facility right here in Northern Ohio? With an impressive body of resources, Decision Point Research can help you in many ways:

- How to identify the jurors who will be responsive to your side as well as those to avoid
- Determine the key questions to ask jurors to guide you in selecting only those jurors who are pre-disposed towards your position
- Identify the key persuasive arguments that will help you win the case
- Minimize unpleasant jury reactions and surprises

When the stakes are high, a mock jury trial is your best defense in your preparation for trial! We specialize in assembling juries that are representative of the jurors you will actually face in the court location of your trial.

Decision Point Research has been helping attorneys win significant jury trials for over 15 years. We know how to conduct mock jury trials that will leverage your success in court.

For your convenience, I've enclosed a return letter and pre-addressed envelope so that you can call or request more information about our services.

Sincerely yours,
Amy Merrill-Boren,
President, Decision Point Research

Figure 28. Mock Trial Letter

The next letter, shown in Fig. 29, includes an invitation to join an exclusive private luncheon/dinner club which carries a considerable amount of prestige and privilege. The invitation presumably appeals to the recipient's ego, a strong psychological motivator for making a purchase.

Since most of the recipients of the letter are leaders of local organizations, the list of recipients is easily compiled for free from LinkedIn, local directories and company websites.

Dear Mr. Doherty,

Did youi know that the University Club is the only private membership dining club of its kind on Tide Point Island?

- The Club is open only to members and not to the general public. As one of our members recently said, "where else can you discuss million-dollar deals?"
- It is a perfect place when you need to entertain business clients or groups in one of our private dining rooms (for breakfast, lunch or late dinner), meet with friends and colleagues, or celebrate an important family event.
- You can also enjoy our exceptional cuisine in our traditionally oak paneled Founder's Room or sample our fine wines or spirits in the atmosphere of our English style Tap Room or beautiful outdoor garden.

As part of a select group of community and executive leaders, I would like to take the liberty of nominating you for membership in the University Club. As a member, you will join a most distinctive group, which includes the County Executive Director and the Owner of Tide Point Bank Corp., to name just a few.

I have arranged for a Special Guest Membership for you for the month of January. During this time, please feel free to stop by and enjoy our dining facilities. In addition, I am enclosing a membership application for you to sign and return to me. In the meantime, if you have any questions, or desire any information about the Club, please feel free to call me directly.

Sincerely,
Ed Welbourne

Figure 29. Club Membership Letter

The market for an exclusive club membership is similar to our next marketing example involving retirement planning services.

The topic of retirement is of interest to people nearing their retirement age and that may entice them to glance at the letter's contents. The letter emphasizes the writer's retirement planning credentials, his company's mission to help new retirees, a host of related benefits, and an offer of a brochure about retirement wealth protection.

Most likely the recipients will open and read the letter since it doesn't look like "junk" mail.

Dear Mr. Jones:

As someone nearing retirement, it's important that you know about the best ways to protect your assets and earning power for the rest of your life.

Here are some key questions that you should be asking yourself

- What kinds of investments today are guaranteed never to decline in value?
- Are you taking advantage of tax laws and IRA rule changes?
- Are your assets safe from creditors, estate taxation, and other problems that could deplete your assets?
- Which investments can yield the retirement income you will need?
- Have you arranged to "stretch" your IRA so that your children or beneficiaries will be financially protected?

I'm John Daniels, President of the Daniels Retirement Group, Inc., located in Melrose, Ohio. I have spent my entire career helping our clients protect their assets, enjoy total peace of mind, avoid investment volatility, and increase their wealth for themselves and their families.

To receive a free copy of our new brochure, "Protecting Your Wealth in Retirement," or to arrange for a free consultation to discuss your retirement needs with us, simply use the enclosed, stamped return letter or call us at 330-555-1212. I look forward to hearing from you.

Sincerely,
John Daniels, Sr.

Figure 30. Retirement Planning Letter

You probably would never think that the type of business described in Figure 31 would ever use a direct marketing promotion. MBA Excavating &Trucking is a small demolition firm that wanted to find new clients and projects. With an eye on high response rates, the company decided to launch a direct mail marketing campaign targeted to those organizations most likely to be in the market for their services.

Since the buyers of demolition services include construction firms, government construction authorities, housing agencies, school construction departments, and the like, the company was able to compile a list of recipients from local and government directories.

Dear Mr. Simms,

Why are some of the largest construction firms and government agencies hiring MBA Excavating to do their demolition and excavating work?

At MBA Excavating, you are always assured that every assignment is completed to your complete satisfaction. We take special pride in using the most modern equipment to get the job done efficiently and cost-effectively.

- Since we own our own equipment, including dump trucks, backhoes, and excavators, we can keep costs low
- We also service and maintain our equipment on a daily basis, so downtime is almost completely avoided
- We are happy to accommodate last minute changes in your plans and schedules
- We can handle any sized project, big or small.
- We are family owned and managed. A member of our management team will always be on site to personally surpervise your projects

Since 1968, MBA has completed many site preparation and demolition projects in the tri-state area, such as numerous housing complexes, apartment buildings, gas stations, educational facilities, and air & marine terminals, etc.

We would be happy to assist you on any project you have – large or small. Please return the enclosed response letter to request additional information, or simply call us at 800-123-1115.

Sincerely,
Harold Welch

Figure 31. From Demolition to Direct Mail

Being able to target recipients precisely via direct mail marketing, increases the likelihood of reaching them, producing results, and staying within one's promotional budget. The campaign for MBA Excavating was successful in producing a good number of new clients and assignments.

Although we usually rely on letters to produce higher response rates, there are times when other promotional formats may be preferred. In business-to-business situations, a memorandum or executive report can also serve as a familiar design for business communication. Sometimes it can be advantageous to contact consumers via postcards, emails or via social media.

Figure 32. Post Card Reminder

For example, a simple postcard was used recently to remind recipients about an important regulatory deadline. The front of the card cautions the recipient about an important filing date for escrow accounts. Those who fail to comply face stiff financial penalties.

One noticeable feature of the mailing is the professional look and design of the postcard. It avoids power words and flashy headlines and states its purpose in a simple, clear-cut fashion. Like the letters shown in this section, the postcard's purpose is communication.

The back of the card lists the benefits of having the sender provide the requisite compliance services to meet the deadline.

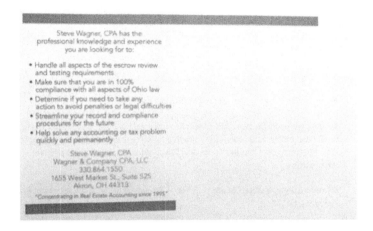

Figure 33. Focus on Benefits

The sender explains how he can safeguard the recipient, and he provides his contact information and address to facilitate a response. Again, the postcard has an air of importance and decorum about it, and it does not look like junk mail.

The accounting firm that sent out the postcards also sent the following letter to part of its target audience to see which would generate a higher response rate. This is typical of "A/B split tests" that are often used in advertising and direct marketing to determine which promotional approach is more effective.

Starting with a question for the recipient was an excellent idea! This engages the recipient immediately and creates a desire for an answer to the question posed in the first paragraph.

The letter goes on to describe the penalties that non-compliance to the new law involves. The writer introduces himself and several bulleted statements to emphasize how he can help the reader. The letter closes with a call to action and an assurance that everything is confidential.

Mr. John Smith
Q&A Title Company
111 Legal Avenue
Akron, Ohio 44334

Dear Mr. Smith:

Are you ready for Ohio's Title Insurance Escrow deadline?

As you know, under Ohio law, Title companies must employ a certified public accountant to review your escrow bank accounts and submit a complete report no later than December 31st. Failure to comply with this law may result in $25,000 fines per violation and/or license revocation.

My name is Steve Wagner, CPA and I can help you comply with the Ohio Title Insurance Escrow lay, by

- Handling all aspects of the escrow review and testing requirements
- Making sure that you are in 100% compliance with all aspects of the Ohio law
- Determining if you need to take any action to avoid penalties or legal difficulties
- Streamlining your record and compliance procedure for the future
- Helping solve any accounting or tax problem quickly and permanentl.

You can call me at 330-864-1550 with any questions or to discuss your escrow accounts or accounting problems that you may have. There is no obligation and your call will be strictly confidential.

Sincerely,
Steve Wagner, CPA

Figure 34. Letter Used in A/B Split Test

One improvement would be to provide a return card or letter for those who do not wish to call but want to request a brochure. Sending the brochure also provides a good reason for a follow-up call. Surprisingly enough, the letter and postcards produced about the same number of replies. When it comes to an important deadline, the calendar warning really works!

Meeting quotas and deadlines are also serious business issues in the realm of personal selling. It's been estimated that there are some 23.3 million salespeople in the top U.S. companies (Williams, 2016).

Here's an example of one sales training company which approached its market via a direct mail letter:

Dear Mr. Klein:

If you would like to see your company achieve this year's sales objectives, a recent interview with Horace Norton, a nationally recognized sales training expert should be of special interest to you.

Recently chosen as one of the nation's top training consultants by Dun's Business Magazine, Mr. Norton discusses
- Sales Incentives – Rewarding an entire sales force of winners
- Telemarketing – Methods to increase sales productivity
- Time Management – New findings, methods and short-cuts
- Prospecting for New Accounts – Raising the "hit ratio"

Many Fortune 500 companies have benefited from Mr. Norton's innovative approach to sales training and sales force motivation. A frequent speaker before the Sales Club of New York, we think you will find Mr. Norton's ideas extremely helpful and valuable.

To obtain a free copy of Mr. Norton's interview, "Achieving Your Company's Sales Objectives," please return the enclosed response letter. There is no obligation.

Sincerely,
Sam Murray

Figure 35. Sales Training Services

This letter addresses the topic from the customer's point of view. It lists compelling benefits, validates important credentials, and suggests an action step to move things forward.

Our last example of a letter in this chapter, shown in Figure 36, involves a promotion for a local car repair shop specializing in European cars.

Dear Mr. Baldwin,

As an owner of an Audi, you undoubtedly appreciate the Audi's unique design and performance which marks the exceptional beauty and quality of European craftsmanship.

Such a fine car deserves a special level of care and maintenance – by people with the knowledge and skill to service your car's requirements and who understand your personal driving needs as well.

At Scheuing Motors, we are European trained mechanics who specialize in the care and maintenance of the Audi automobile:

- *We have been catering to Audi owners for 25 years.*
- *We use the right tools and can fix any problem you may have to protect your factory warranty.*
- *Our periodic service can help protect your factory warranty.*
- *Simply put, we believe that "European craftsmanship is best maintained by European craftsmen."*

I have taken the liberty of enclosing a return letter and stamped envelope by which you can arrange for an evaluation appointment with us for your Audi. In addition, please feel free to call if you'd like to ask any questions about our Audi service or to make an appointment at this time.

Sincerely,
Xavier Bradford

Figure 36. European Car Letter

This letter successfully positions the auto repair shop mechanics as uniquely qualified experts who can provide a high level of professional service. It also coined a new tagline for the company: "European craftsmanship is best maintained by European craftsmen." The result of this successful mailing was a long line of cars lined up around the repair shop the next morning by car owners seeking immediate service.

Due to overwhelming response, the company quickly reduced the quantity of its weekly promotional mailings in order to accommodate the needs of its new clients.

Personalized Direct Mail Brochures

Three things are inevitable in this world: death, taxes and brochures.

In general, people like brochures and they develop an emotional attachment to their colorful look, "warm and fuzzy" feel and entertaining content. The brochure can go to great lengths in praising the company and its products, thereby reinforcing a company's message to prospects, customers, and employees.

Salespeople find that brochures reinforce their message and help to close sales. From their viewpoint, brochures are indispensable sales tools that can help convince prospects to make a purchase. At the same time, the loyalty of existing customers may be strengthened by a brochure's persuasive message.

Brochures may also be useful for bolstering the morale and confidence of one's own employees. The brochure provides a quality image and reassurance about concerns that employees may have. It does this, in part, by disseminating the same positive information throughout the organization so that everyone is "on the same page."

As shown on the next page, the Audi repair shop in the previous section prepared a simple tri-fold brochure. The three cover panels of this consumer-oriented brochure are quite simple, with the middle panel reiterating the firm's unique capabilities, and the back cover reminding us of the company's European heritage.

The inside panels include comments from three existing customers. These personal endorsements are extremely valuable. Prospective customers will likely treat personal observations as highly credible and influential. Testimonials from existing customers, local government leaders, or well-known business people and citizens strengthen the company's promotions and make them more convincing.

Figure 37A. Tri-Fold Brochure (Cover Panels)

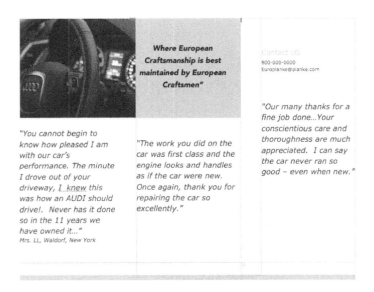

Where European
Craftsmanship is best
maintained by European
Craftsmen"

Contact US
800-000-0000
Europlanke@planke.com

"You cannot begin to
know how pleased I am
with our car's
performance. The minute
I drove out of your
driveway, I knew this
was how an AUDI should
drive!. Never has it done
so in the 11 years we
have owned it..."
Mrs. LL, Waldorf, New York

"The work you did on the
car was first class and the
engine looks and handles
as if the car were new.
Once again, thank you for
repairing the car so
excellently."

"Our many thanks for a
fine job done...Your
conscientious care and
thoroughness are much
appreciated. I can say
the car never ran so
good – even when new."

Figure 37B. Tri-Fold Brochure (Inside Panels)

One of the reasons for using the tri-fold format is that it is an inexpensive brochure to create. The company in this example used Microsoft Word to create the brochure that is shown. With Microsoft Word, photographs, graphics, and other images can by inserted. Different colors and fonts make the brochure writing task doable,

The tri-fold can be printed in any color by a laser printer on 8" x 11" printer paper, either plain or glossy. Once folded, the brochure can be inserted into a business envelope and mailed upon request with a transmittal note or letter. Alternatively, the brochure can be downloaded as a pdf file, or offered with more information via a customized website landing page.

The next brochure, developed by the author of this book, offers an important topic for anyone selling a product or service: "How to Find New Customers." This is a universal question that every organization must answer to be successful.

Figure 38. Brochure Cover

The graphic image on the brochure cover of the dollar sign in the middle of a maze suggests that a new customer solution may be illusive. However, it also implies that the contents of the brochure may solve this particular puzzle.

The brochure uses a Question and Answer format to present information to its readers. This is a versatile format that can be used in many ways. For example, it can be used to present an interview with a chief executive officer or other key company executive. It provides a uniform message for the rest of the organization to follow. In addition, it answers many common questions that readers may have and thus creates an immediate bond with them.

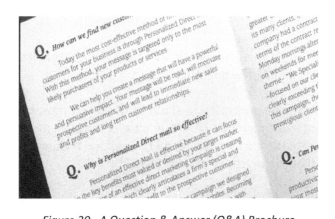

Figure 39. A Question & Answer (Q&A) Brochure

An accounting firm mailed the following six-page brochure (using a Q&A format) to law firms in the Northeast informing them about a new IRS program targeting attorneys with in-depth income tax audits. To reduce expense, the brochure was only mailed to attorneys who requested it.

The brochure is simple and straight-forward and was relatively inexpensive to prepare. It looks classy, informative and professional. No junk mail here!

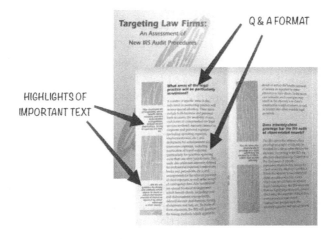

Figure 40. Q&A Brochure Example

Brochures add a great amount of utility and value that helps motivate and influence potential buyers.

We advocate one principal rule about brochures: in most cases, you should not mail brochures with your initial promotion. Brochures only increase the package weight and, therefore, the amount of postage that you must pay to Uncle Sam.

If you only send brochures upon request, you have eliminated sending brochures to non-interested individuals. In essence, you have narrowed down your list, so that you can now concentrate on your most likely buyers (e.g., those individuals who have responded). You have eliminated a considerable amount of waste, and perhaps saved a good number of trees!

Telemarketing

Some people dream of making "first contact" with aliens on Mars. For earthbound marketers, one of the critical steps in direct marketing also involves "first contact." Every mailing produces a response rate, perhaps from 1% or less for junk mail to 5% or more for a more personalized approach. Depending on the quantities mailed, the marketer is soon holding on to numerous replies that require some action.

Most of the products and services discussed in this book (e.g., new swimming pools, car repairs, legal and accounting services, apartment rentals) involve telephone contacts leading to face-to-face discussions with the prospective buyers. In general, the higher the price of the offering, and the more personal sales and/or service is involved, the greater the need for personal contact.

Suffice it to say that no calls are necessary for products that you can routinely fulfill without any contact.

Individuals will usually request a copy of your brochure, while others will ask to be contacted by telephone. In _both_ cases, you should plan on calling the individual. Obviously, you would need to wait a few days to be certain that your brochure has been received if the person requested it.

Note that you should not call or pursue individuals who have not responded to your promotion. Some marketers and sales managers advocate calling everyone on the mailing list, even if they have not responded to the mailing. That is a waste of time and effort and it defeats the entire purpose of direct mail marketing which is designed to _identify likely buyers._

You need to have a telemarketing plan in place so that you can reach out to the individuals who have indicated an interest in your offering. These are now your most likely prospects, and you need to devote 100% of your effort towards converting them into buyers!

Telemarketing can be a simple process if you keep one thing in mind. The sole purpose of the call is to secure a meeting with the prospective buyer. Selling takes place during the face-to-face meeting. You should not try to sell anything over the telephone. Your only objective is to ask for is an appointment, and you can suggest at least two alternative dates and times so that a mutually convenient meeting can be agreed upon.

Most campaigns produce a good number of calls that need to be made. It helps if the calls are divided among the salespeople or others within the office. Meetings with each prospect can be arranged for colleagues who are located in the vicinity of the individuals being called.

Here's a sample telemarketing worksheet and script. Although you can expect some no's, it's also a wonderful feeling when the person on the phone agrees to meet with you.

Prospect's Name:	Hello, Mr./Mrs._____
Caller's Name	This is _____ calling from the ABC Company. I'm calling to make sure that you received our brochure about the new carpeting for your home. We just finished installing carpeting at the Jones' house across the street. Did you have any questions concerning the brochure?
Show interest	May I ask, how many rooms are you thinking of carpeting? How old are your existing carpets?
Remind them of savings and benefits	You know, when ABC does the installation, you get 45% off the retail price! Quite a savings! And you still get our Lifetime Warranty!
Sound cheerful and upbeat!	My associate, Bill Jones, will be in your neighborhood next Tues. He can stop by at 10AM in the morning or 2PM in the afternoon to show you some samples and take some measurements. Which time is best for you?
Confirm Appointment	OK, Bill Jones will see you around _____AM/PM at your house to go over some samples. I know you will be delighted with the styl and high-quality of our wool carpets.
Closing	I enjoyed talking with you. Have a great weekend!

Figure 41. Sample Telemarketing Script

Summary

This chapter has focused on some of the best practices in personalized direct mail marketing. Most companies find that direct mail is extremely versatile and can be used to tackle almost any kind of product and/or service promotion.

The "secret" to achieving exceptional direct marketing results is to know your market and understand the viewpoint and needs of the recipient. There is no magic formula. Every direct marketing promotion must be able to offer some benefit to the recipient that they value and need for themselves or their business.

The examples of direct mail campaigns from a variety of businesses demonstrate the power that a simple and straight forward letter and plain envelope can have. By dispensing with the usual glitz and attention getting gimmicks, respondents are sure to open, read, and act upon your direct mail marketing efforts.

We reviewed a few simple brochures, with the tri-fold being suggested as a low-cost brochure that can be designed and printed using Microsoft Word. Typically, the brochure is not sent with the original promotional letter but is offered as something that can be requested. This avoids the extra bulk, weight and extra printing and postage costs that would be necessary if the brochure were mailed to your entire mailing list. It is much more economical to mail the brochure just to those respondents who request it!

Finally, we reviewed plans to call individuals who responded to your mailing. The objective in most cases is to set a date and time for a face-to-face meeting. The individuals who have responded have the greatest potential of becoming your new buyers. The direct mail marketing campaign has identified these individuals, and it has helped to warm them up for the selling process.

Chapter 4 addresses an important question: How do copy-writers know what to say? What should be written in our promotional materials? Do we have copy guidelines that work, or are we forced back into the junk mail jungle again looking for power words or expressions?

We will also explore some incredible technological solutions that can guide the creative writing process as well as our direct marketing strategies.

Action Steps

At some point, telephone calls must be made to the individuals who respond to your promotion. It's a good idea to prepare a script and practice making some mock telemarketing calls in your office.

If possible, try to set up some practice sessions in your office to help train your team of telemarketers. You can use different situations to see how well calls might go with different types of customers, such as customers who appear hesitant, distrusting, unhappy, argumentative, or even silent (Saunders, 2018). Discussion of these situations can be invaluable before actual calls are made.

Remember that your objective is to secure face-to-face meetings, and not to sell anything over the telephone.

After a few tries, you will probably find that with some practice, telemarketing can be an enjoyable and rewarding experience!

CHAPTER 4

KNOWING WHAT TO SAY TO YOUR CUSTOMERS

> *"Everyone has their own ways of*
> *expression. I believe we all have a lot to*
> *say but finding ways to say it is more*
> *than half the battle."*

Criss Jami, (2011)
American Poet

Writing promotional materials is both an art and a science. What one writes has to be crisp, clear, informative and persuasive. It has to offer a plausible and rational basis for buying, and it must also strike an emotional cord with the recipient. Through some sort of alchemy, the copywriter has to produce something that people will want to read and act upon.

There are basically two approaches in writing direct mail materials. The most common method is to develop new creatives based on consumer research. The new challenger creatives are then tested (in A/B split tests) against copy that performed well previously. In essence, this is a trial and error approach, in which alternative copy platforms are tested during a live promotional campaign. Personal judgment based on experience and market familiarity come into play when there are no clear-cut creative winners.

The second approach uses a statistical method, called "conjoint analysis" to assign positive and negative utility values for each product or service feature. Using survey data, conjoint analysis tells us if consumers like or dislike product or service elements or characteristics (price, size, performance, prestige, style, availability, image, and so forth). Based on these results, conjoint analysis can identify the optimal message that we should use in our promotional materials.

The purpose of this chapter it to introduce conjoint analysis to you, as well as two alternative ways of conducting a conjoint study. One statistical software package, aptly named, XLSTAT, since It uses Microsoft Excel, can empower you or your organization to conduct a "do-it-yourself" conjoint study in a relatively low-cost manner. Anyone who is familiar with Excel, and is capable of collecting survey data, can run conjoint analysis using XLSTAT. We'll look at XLSTAT in more detail shortly.

There are other conjoint analysis approaches, such as IdeaMap™ and Addressable Minds™ developed by Howard R. Moskowitz, Ph.D., that have been widely used in the packaged food and other industries. Many companies often seek out Dr. Moskowitz and the services of his marketing research company that specializes in conjoint analysis research. Although more expensive, oftentimes having experts on board who design the survey, and perform all statistical analyses, as well as provide interpretation of the results, more than compensates for the added expense.

Conjoint Analysis 101

Although we collect a substantial amount of information about people, such as purchasing behavior (product usage, brand loyalty, product attitudes), demographics (age, gender, income), psychographics (social class, lifestyle type, personality traits), and behavior (product usage, brand loyalty, product-related attitudes), none of these variables tells us what to say to one's customers or prospects.

As noted above, we may run A/B split tests to determine if a particular creative outperforms other creatives in the marketplace. In addition, we may compare alternative creative approaches in focus groups in an attempt to see if a sample of consumers prefers one creative platform over another.

Conjoint analysis fills a critical gap in direct marketing. In Conjoint analysis, various product or service features are considered jointly or simultaneously, which approximates the way in which people think and rank product and service attributes. We can identify the product features that people prefer and to which they would respond positively.

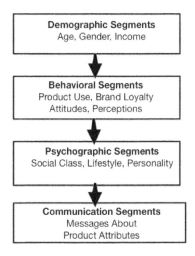

Figure 42. The Evolution of Segmentation:
Identifying Unique Communication Segments

This statistical approach allows us to identify unique consumer segments – and communicate to those segments – using the product attributes that consumers value most highly.

Brand Name	Price	Color	Style	Image
Mercedes	$80,000	Red	Sports	Prestige
Audi	$50,000	White	Sedan	Performance
BMW	$60,000	Black	Convertible	Youthful
Porsche	$75,000	White	2-seater	Sporty

Table 2. Product Attributes Used in Conjoint Analysis Example

For example, Table 2 shows a number of variables about autos (price, color, style, image, and brand name) that we wish to test to see which combination consumers prefer.

Survey respondents are shown combinations or pairs of product descriptions and asked to decide which item (A or B) they would buy, from the given choices. They repeat making choices for 20 or more additional screens. Based on the survey answers, the conjoint software determines the optimal combinations of product characteristics that different consumer group desire.

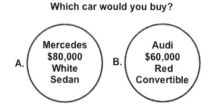

Figure 43. Paired Comparison Question

In addition to using product features or characteristics, we also need to discover which emotional dimensions the consumer associates with the product or service in question. Most product and service purchases tend to be made on a qualitative or emotional basis. The survey presents statements of perceptions that echo what the consumer may be feeling or thinking. For research purposes, these perceptions can be generated via in-house brainstorming, by surveys, or by focus groups using consumer participants.

Emotional Perceptions:

I feel good when others notice me driving

I feel like I've made it

Brand Perceptions:

America's most trusted dealer

Unparalleled luxury

Product Perceptions

All the technology you could ever want

The best safety record in the industry

Figure 44. Examples of Consumer Perceptions

The process is also visual, so that visual images of people buying or using the product or service are shown in order to capture the product's use in a social setting," be it a gift or purchase.

Based on the above elements and levels, consumers are shown a series of computer screens of different grouped or conjoined elements. The purpose of the survey is to identify those elements (statements and images) that the consumer views positively vs. those viewed negatively. In this way, we can predict which promotional appeals will be welcomed vs. those that will be rejected or ignored.

The following image shows a typical screen format used to survey respondents in Dr. Moskowitz's IdeaMap^{TM} (IdeaMap^{TM} screens and information used with permission of Howard A. Moskowitz, Ph.D.):

Sample Research Screen Shown To Respondents

Nobody knows more about car performance than the German craftsmen at Audi

I can always find a car in my price range at the Audi dealer

No one knows more about car performance than Audi's mechanics

I think Audi is one of the safest cars on the highway

How well does this describe a car you want to buy?
1 = EXTREMELY WELL .... 9 = NOT AT ALL

Figure 45. Example of IdeaMap™ Question Format

From this process, utility values of each of the above elements and levels can be calculated. The results of the conjoint analysis can identify those product and service attributes the consumer views favorably, as well as those viewed neutrally or negatively.

The results of a financial services consumer study generated by IdeaMap™ are shown below. The statements are grouped by average score. In this case, the top or "A" portion of the table reflects utility scores of 1 to 4 and contains product or service dimensions rated positively and therefore highly valued by consumers. These statements should be the ones featured in any direct promotion.

The "B" or middle section of the table reflects statements with utility scores of zero and are perceived as neutral. Consumers would be indifferent to these promotional statements, and they would neither motivate nor dissuade consumers from buying.

The statements in the "C" or bottom area of the table reflect utility scores of minus 1 to minus 4. Consumers reacted unfavorably to these statements which would, therefore, "turn off" prospective buyers. These statements should be avoided in any promotional effort.

ID	Statement	Score	Type
1	Smart cards that no one else can use	4	Pos
2	Eye or finger scanning security safeguards	4	Pos
3	Priority customers receive priority level service	3	Pos
4	Free assessment of year end financial situation	3	Pos
5	Access to tax shelters to minimize income taxes	3	Pos
6	Manage investments via cloud from any device	2	Pos
7	A personal banker who knows your goals	2	Pos
8	Attend our free financial planning workshops	2	Pos
9	Connect online in real time to a customer rep	0	Neutral
10	Faster online loan application process	0	Neutral
11	Reps can help determine the services needed	0	Neutral
12	Make appointments online for branch meeting	0	Neutral
13	Kiosks provide access to manage investments	0	Neutral
14	Evening and weekend hours for convenience	0	Neutral
15	24-hour access available at many locations	-1	Avoid
16	Personal assistance available 24 hours a day	-2	Avoid
17	No ATM fees at or bank or theirs	-2	Avoid
18	Receive 10% discount with new credit application	-3	Avoid
19	Banking transactions can be done at any branch	-4	Avoid
20	Keep minimum balances for free bank accounts	-4	Avoid

Table 3. IdeaMap™ Results

Conjoint analysis should be a revelation for marketers and copywriters alike, since it can guide us with the optimal message to a particular segment.

Based on the utility values, conjoint analysis can show which combination of statements would have an optimal utility value among consumers. By following the recommendations in the above table, the marketer experienced a 42% increase in response rate and a sales lift of $1339/K.

What a feeling!
A car of unparalleled luxury!
And Performance!

Figure 46. An Optimal IdeaMap^{TM} Solution

Interestingly, the survey respondents may not have seen the winning combination of statements and images together, but the conjoint program can compute which statements and images would make the most powerful impact if grouped together. The above combination of elements reinforces the image of a woman who is youthful, sophisticated, sensual and resourceful.

This ability to bring together lifestyle dimensions and perceptions represents the ultimate marriage of marketing communications and research technology.

Conjoint Analysis with Excel

XLSTAT is a statistical computer program for Microsoft Excel that performs over 200 statistical routines and features, including conjoint analysis. This section will review this product in some detail, since it allows us to conduct a complete conjoint study at a reasonable cost. All the screen shots of the XLSTAT software are used with the permission of Addinsoft, Paris, France.

The first screen shown below is what a participant taking a conjoint study survey would see. In the example below, the participant is being asked to make a choice and indicate which credit card they would find most attractive.

Addinsoft.2018. XLSTAT 2018. Data Analysis and Statistical Solution for Microsoft Excel. Paris.

Table 4. Sample XLSTAT Screen of Product Variables

In the above example, there are ten different variables showing the different brand choices available. One of the strengths of conjoint analysis is that it considers different combinations of product or service characteristics simultaneously, rather than viewing each characteristic in isolation from one another. When choosing to buy a product, there is always some trade-off involved. We like card #3 because it has no annual fee compared to the other cards. But to get that card, we would have to pay a higher interest rate on balances, as well as give up cash back on our purchases.

Aggregated utilities:

Source	Utilities
Temperature-Ice	-0,077
Temperature-Very warm	0,091
Temperature-Warm	-0,014
Sugar-1 sugar	0,107
Sugar-2 sugar	0,006
Sugar-No sugar	-0,113
Lemon-no	0,025
Lemon-yes	-0,025
Intensity-Low	0,072
Intensity-Medium	0,074
Intensity-Strong	-0,146

Aggregated importances:

Source	Importances
Temperature	25,643
Sugar	33,372
Lemon	7,488
Intensity	33,497

Addinsoft.2018. XLSTAT 2018. Data Analysis and Statistical Solution for Microsoft Excel. Paris.

Table 5. Product Utilities & Importance

The chart above indicates the utility scores and relative importance of variables in a recent food study. It's easy to see in this example that the two characteristics scoring highest among consumers are associated with (taste) Intensity and sugar levels (sweetness). This information is essential in deciding on product composition as well as what to say to potential buyers in the market.

The following barchart shows a view of conjoint utility scores, with negative utility ratings to the left and positive utility ratings to the right. The length of the bars represents the size of the utility rating, or the perceptual importance to the survey respondents.

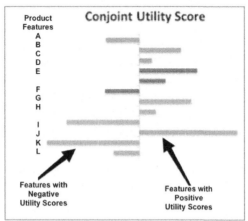

Addinsoft. 2018. Solution for Microsoft Excel. Paris, France. Used with permission

Figure 47. Magnitude of Conjoint Utility Scores

It's clear in this example that Feature "J" evoked the largest positive rating of any feature, while feature "K" scored the most negative.

At this point, we are beginning to get some idea about the features that are important to the market as well as those that cause a negative or adverse reaction.

A data input screen for XLSTAT is shown below. Each variable is listed on a column with their respective choice elements underneath. Variables can be easily added or removed, thereby reducing the overall learning curve for assembling the survey and for analyzing data.

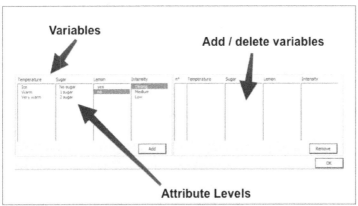

Addinsoft.2018. XLSTAT 2018. Data Analysis and Statistical Solution for Microsoft Excel. Paris Used with permission.

Table 6. Sample XLSTAT Screen

The Message & Theme

Armed with the conjoint analysis results, we now have more insight about the communications that we should be using to motivate our audience. But we are not there yet. Although we know the product and service characteristics that will be very well received (as well as elements to avoid promoting), we're not quite ready to send off our campaign just yet. We need to go one step further and identify our USP or unique selling proposition.

What is it that makes our company and/or product special? What sets us apart from our competitors? It may be a capability they don't have, a feature or benefit that is unique to our offering, or some aspect of our service that we do better than anyone else. The point is that we need to be able to determine what is that we do so well.

As famed marketer, Leo Burnett, once noted, "every product has drama inherently in it" (Burnett, 1960). That drama or excitement is what differentiates us from everybody else. Our core competencies provide advantages over every other product or service that competes with us. Therefore, we need to develop a statement that expresses our unique advantages and benefits. The first task is to gather information about the organization and what it does.

Remember the European car repair shop we looked at previously? (See Chapter 3, page 66). A researcher visited the shop to see if any uniqueness could be detected. While walking around the repair shop, the researcher observed something that was very odd: every mechanic was speaking German. No one who worked there would have realized that anything unusual was going on. But to the researcher, the fact that the repair shop focused on German automobiles, turned his visit into an "A-HA!" moment, and it helped to articulate the firm's uniqueness, e.g., that "European craftsmanship is best maintained by European craftsmen." It has been the company's tagline or slogan ever since.

Another example also illustrates how important it is to identify a company's "essence" to communicate its competitive advantage to prospective customers. This firm, which provided janitorial and building maintenance services, needed to convey its ability to satisfy customers to a greater extent than its competitors. Among its many clients, including banks, theaters, and hospitals, the company also had a contract to clean a National Guard Armory. The terms of the contract were very demanding and required that the premises be spotless on the Monday morning after several thousand soldiers used the facility during the previous weekend for meetings, drills and practice. The resulting theme – "We specialize in Cleaning High Traffic Areas" – exceeded the needs of most customers. As a result of this direct marketing campaign, the company added many large and prestigious clients. Among the new clients, at the time, was the World Trade Center.

Another service example again proves how important it is to have a unique selling proposition. In this case, an investment management firm was trying to discover what to say to prospective clients that would differentiate it from all other Wall Street financial companies. Advertisements in the investment community tend to promise the same thing, e.g., to customize their strategy for each client, to grow or maintain the portfolio value, to take advantage of new investment opportunities, and to safeguard the account from taxes and preventable losses. However, another "A-Ha!" moment changed all of that. In a discussion with the firm's top executives, they mentioned that what they really wanted was to "become each client's family office." The direct marketing firm developed a new promotional platform using this statement, since it was an ideal tagline for the firm's future promotional efforts.

Finally, here's an example where a "gimmick" actually helped strengthen a wholesale marketing strategy. The company, a well-known rug manufacturer, wanted to expand its retail network. It sent out notices to independent rug stores across the country indicating that it was sending each of them a truck load of rugs to see which products could be featured in their stores. Store managers were at first apprehensive about receiving a large truck load that they did not order nor want. What actually arrived at each store was a diecast 1/64 scale model truck complete with miniature carpet samples. An exception to the rule about avoiding "gimmicks," this promotion created good will and helped to add several new dealers to the company's distribution network. No doubt the company could have created a tagline about "truckloads of carpet choices" if they wanted to extend the campaign.

Figure 48. 1/64 Scale Diecast Tractor Trailer ca 1988

Taglines express the unique benefits or capability that a brand offers within the marketplace. To create a tagline, it's usually helpful to investigate all of the Features, Advantages and Benefits (FAB's) that the brand offers. The FAB approach, a mainstay of the marketing profession for many years, can lead directly to benefit statements and taglines of immense promotional value. Using this approach, you can either brainstorm or conduct research to develop a list of the dimensions for FAB analysis.

A completed example of a FAB worksheet appears below. The worksheet demonstrates how FAB is used to understand the important characteristics of a brand (product or service) in developing potential communications to consumers. In this case, a tagline is also produced.

FEATURES	ADVANTAGES	BENEFITS
(Physical components)	(What each component does)	(Benefits to the consumer)
Ergonomic design	Rest hands on padded area	Less fatigue; use longer hours
Removable screen	Screen detaches, use w/o keypad	Use as tablet
Built in 110 & 220 power	US & Foreign compatible	*Travel ready for US & the world*
Molded one-piece design	Protects computer from damage	Strong & almost indestructible
Long lasting battery	Runs 12 hours without charging	No down-time, interruptions
PC & Mac compatible	Can run mac & pc programs	1 device, saves $, use best PC or mac programs

Table 7. FAB Example

Based on the FAB analysis, we see that this product offers a host of significant characteristics with marketing potential. For example, the following tagline offers a unique way to position this product: "A Computer that's made to travel the world." You can easily imagine promotional materials and advertisements showing the computer being used in exotic and remote locations, perhaps even on top of Mt. Everest!

It can be very helpful to review your brand name also to see what specific perceptions and emotions it evokes. Are they positive or negative? Do consumers have any strong reactions when they hear the brand name or see your logo? Now is the time to determine if you still have a stellar reputation and image. Focus groups can be a good way to uncover both positive and negative associations, rather than conducting a more elaborate, full-scale survey. Focus group participants may say something of profound value that becomes the company's future tagline.

Summary

Chapter 4 has addressed the problem of determining what to say or write to prospective customers. The chapter introduced a number of technological tools that can help simplify and improve the process of creating and writing direct mail marketing copy. Among these technologies are Conjoint measurement, such as Dr. Howard Moskowitz's Ideamap™ and the XLstat™ software package for Microsoft Excel.

The importance of the message or theme cannot be overemphasized. Techniques were suggested for identifying one's unique selling proposition (USP) characteristics as derived from consumers or brainstormed internally. These may lead to your developing a company tagline or slogan, which is a powerful expression that captures the essence of what the company and its products stand for.

Chapter 5 turns to the question of identifying our best customers and prospects. Before we send out any promotions, we again need to utilize some computer programs that will help us target and deliver our messages effectively.

Action Steps

Here's an opportunity to look more closely at the brand that you are marketing. Imagine that you are a marketing consultant looking to improve a product or service offering. Please complete the following FAB analysis worksheet which will help you determine the factors that contribute to your brand's uniqueness.

Please use the following FAB worksheet to list the Features, Advantages and Benefits that are inherent in your Brand.

Company: _____
Industry: _____
Brand: _____

FEATURES	ADVANTAGES	BENEFITS
(Physical components)	(What each component does)	(Benefits to the consumer)

Table 8. FAB Worksheet

Once the FAB analysis has been completed, you now have the opportunity to be especially creative! What unique characteristics did you notice? Are there benefits that can translate into a tagline? Feel free to use the examples in this chapter for inspiration!

CHAPTER 5

IDENTIFYING YOUR BEST CUSTOMERS

In 1980, Bankers Trust Company, one of the largest Commercial Banks in the world, did an extraordinary thing. They divested themselves of nearly all of their retail branches in New York City, leaving themselves with a handful of branches in and around the Borough of Manhattan. After studying their customer base for many years, the bank's management team had concluded that 80% of the bank's profits came from just 20% of its clientele, whose personal and business accounts were situated in just 12 branches. They were deemed to be the bank's best and wealthiest clients. Within four years of this decision, the bank's profits soared to record levels.

Despite the existence of sophisticated customer databases today, many companies still fail to focus on their most important customers. The reasons for this are simple: many companies don't know who their best customers are, nor do they know how to identify them.

This chapter focuses on existing customers, and why we want to target our mailings to our best customers. It's assumed that you maintain your list of clients in some sort of database, whether it is an Excel worksheet, Microsoft Access Database, or more sophisticated Oracle Database. If not, perhaps this chapter will inspire you to start organizing your client records more thoroughly, if only to capitalize on the marketing methods being presented.

Acquiring lists to mail to *new* or *prospective* customers will be discussed in the next chapter as part of Direct Mail Production.

Computing RFM Scores

Let's begin by looking at the records of ten existing customers in our database:

Cust. ID	# Months	R	#Trip	F	$	M	RFM	R+F+M
540	4	5	8	5	1280	5	555	15
288	5	5	1	1	45	1	511	7
778	15	3	6	5	2100	5	355	13
088	12	4	2	1	375	2	412	7
676	18	3	1	1	75	1	311	5
779	23	3	3	2	475	3	323	8
002	3	5	5	4	1650	5	545	14
415	30	2	2	1	135	1	211	4
655	23	3	4	3	350	2	332	8
706	5	5	5	2	450	3	523	13

Table 9. Sample of Customer RFM Scores

To identify the best customers in the database, we use an RFM model, based on three customer characteristics: Recency (When did they last buy?); Frequency (How often did they buy?); and Monetary Value (How much did they spend?). Each customer in the database is scored and sorted by their RFM scores, from highest to lowest. The best customers have the highest RFM scores, indicating that they shopped most recently, are frequent shoppers, and they spent the most. The scores for each characteristic run from 5 (best) to 1 (worst).

Listed in Table 10, we see the rating scales used in computing the above RFM scores. Note that the scales of each RFM factor can change depending on the industry or product. For example, for a new automobile, the monetary spending range would be considerably higher; frequency could reflect the number of autos bought previously; and recency could refer to the last date the customer brought in their current auto for servicing.

Recency (Last Visit)	R		Frequency (# Visits)	F	Monetary Spending	M
6 months or less	5		5 visits or more	5	$1000 or more	5
7 to 12 months	4		4	4	$550 to $999	4
11 to 24 months	3		3	3	$450 to $549	3
25 to 36 months	2		2	2	$350 to $449	2
36 months or more	1		1	1	$1 to $349	1

Table 10. RFM Rating Scales

Although based on purchasing history, RFM is a valuable predictor of future shopping patterns for most consumers.   If we examine frequency distributions for past mailings in each of the RFM cells, we will typically see results as follows:

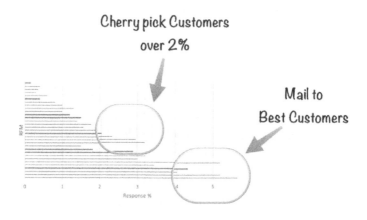

Figure 49. RFM Frequency Distribution of Response Rates

Customers in the highest RFM cells typically have the highest response rates to our mailings.

As shown in Figure 49, historical response data can often aid us in identifying customers who have lower RFM scores but who also responded relatively well to past mailings. This gives us an opportunity to "cherry pick" those customers by "forcing" them into future mailings. By including those customers, total response rates and revenue will improve for future mailings.

Some companies also deem it appropriate to combine the RFM score by using R+F+M. By doing this, customers with higher spending may receive greater emphasis than they would normally receive due to lower R or F scores. It makes excellent sense to focus on high value customers (with high "M" scores) since they tend to outspend other customers. By doing so, the company may be able to reactivate these "big spenders," such as customer #778 (see Table 9 above), despite the fact that this customer has not visited a store recently.

R+F+M also gives us an additional opportunity to examine the stability of existing customer segments in the database to determine if customer attrition or "churn" is occurring, e.g., whether we are holding on to our best customers or losing them. By regrouping the combined R+F+M scores into Value Segments (Highest, High, Medium, and Low), we can view a simple summary of attrition from one time period to another.

Theoretically, it should be easier and less costly to retain an existing customer than attract a new client who is either unfamiliar with our brand or who is already satisfied with another company's product or service. By analyzing the RFM scores of existing customers, we should be able to identify customers who have become inactive and who need our immediate attention to reactivate them.

Customers Who
Decreased in Value
(Above & right of diagonal)

2015	2018 Highest Value	High Value	Medium Value	Low Value	Lost?
Highest Value	20%	20%	15%	15%	30%
High Value	15	15	20	15	35
Medium Value	15	15	20	15	35
Low Value	10	15	25	20	25
New	25	20	30	25	

Customers Who
Increased in Value
(Below & left of diagonal)

Table 11A. Changes in Customer Value
(Value based on R+F+M Score)

What we see are both gains and losses. The areas below and left of the diagonal indicate customers who have gained in value (shopped more often or spent more) from 2015 to 2018; while areas above and to the right of the diagonal shows a decline in value (e.g., customers who shopped less often or spent less) from 2015 to 2018. Customers along the diagonal are unchanged.

By 2018, only 20% of the highest valued customers in 2015 remained in that group. Reading horizontally, by 2018, 20% of the highest valued customers were now classified as High; 15% moved down to Medium Value; and 15% became Low. For the High Value customer group, 15% remained High, and 15% were also upsold to Very High; however, 20% fell to Medium; and 15% fell to Low.

Customers who fell in value (particularly from Highest Value to a lower category) could be offered Incentives, such as receiving a coupon or offering loyalty club membership benefits. For those customers who are no longer buying or appear to be lost or inactive (a whopping 30% of Highest customers from 2015), there may be an opportunity to reactivate them via promotional contact using mail or email.

Changes in customer value can also be viewed using decile analysis, dividing the database into 10 deciles. Here's an excerpt from a company's top 5 deciles:

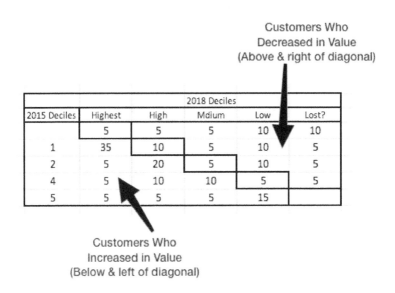

2015 Deciles	Highest	High	Mdium	Low	Lost?
	5	5	5	10	10
1	35	10	5	10	5
2	5	20	5	10	5
4	5	10	10	5	5
5	5	5	5	15	

Customers Who
Decreased in Value
(Above & right of diagonal)

Customers Who
Increased in Value
(Below & left of diagonal)

*Table 11B. Decile Analysis of Customer Value Changes
(% Changes from 2015 to 2018)*

In some ways, decile analysis may provide a greater ability to identify and track consumer changes since the consumers are homogeneous within their respective deciles. By grouping customers who behave similarly, we can use A/B split tests to compare a standard promotional mailer vs. challengers (e.g., new creative approaches) that offer different creatives, prices, products, or copy messages to see if there is any impact on each decile, and whether any response lift or sales increase occurs.

We turn next to two remaining statistical approaches for identifying customer segments that helps us determine what to say and to whom to say it.

Factor Analysis Segmentation

The first statistical approach is a powerful multivariate procedure, called Factor Analysis. Factor Analysis allows us to go beyond purchasing behavior and demographics, which are the segmentation approaches frequently used. Instead, Factor Analysis allows us to segment the consumer database according to *psychographics* (e.g., attitudes and perceptions), which helps to give us insights into what the consumer is thinking and feeling.

Factor Analysis works by grouping people together who have similar answers to attitudinal survey questions. Thus, we can identify those individuals who appear to be homogeneous (similar) within their respective groups, but who are different or are heterogenous (dissimilar) with respect to people in other groups.

By having similar attitudes, people within a particular attitudinal segment tend to respond the same way to marketing proposals that interest them. This happens because people with similar answers tend to behave similarly in terms of preferring and buying products.

To conduct Factor Analysis, a survey is administered to a sample of consumers to gather the necessary *psychographic* information. Respondents indicate their agreement or disagreement with attitudinal statements using a 5 point scale (from 5, highly agree to 1, highly disagree).

Table 12 shows the statements that were used to identify consumer segments using Factor Analysis in an automobile study. These statements were shown in combination with photos and other images to identify an optimal message, e.g., one which produces the highest positive rating among alternative promotional messages.

#		Score
1	I only shop for an Audi when I need a new car	
2	I deserve to reward myself by shopping for a new car	
3	I feel closer to another person when we go car shopping	
4	I don't like pushy car salesmen	
5	I look for new car bargains whenever I can	
6	I feel good when I am driving my new Audi	
7	I wish buying a car was a lot more fun	
8	I usually dress well when I go shopping at an Audi dealer	
9	I feel good when people notice my new Audi	
10	Auto shopping is stressful	
11	I go back to dealers who know how to treat customers well	
12	I'd love to buy an Audi for my spouse	
13	I always shop for the best new car value in town	
14	Shopping for a car is a special experience	
15	I like car dealers who appreciate European designs	

Table 12. Sample Survey Statements for Factor Analysis

Based on the answers to the survey, Factor Analysis produces a table of significant factors that exist. In statistical parlance, this means that each factor explains a certain amount of variability (or variance) within the data. With this information, we can formulate promotional messages that correspond to the mindsets of each consumer segment.

Factor Analysis is a relatively easy statistical technique to use. There are a number of statistical packages available today, such as SAS, SPSS and XLSTAT, as well as Excel templates that include factor analysis routines. In addition, you can also perform factor analysis on your iPhone or iPad with a mobile statistical package, such as StatSuite.

In each of the following factors, the consumer responses (to the statements in Table 12) have been grouped together to form a number of segments in which members share similar attitudes.

#1	#2	#3	#4	#5	#6	#1 Self-Absorbed Shopper
x						I deserve to reward myself by shopping for a car
x						I feel good when I am driving my new Audi
x						I feel good when people notice my new Audi
						#2 Relationship Shopper
	x					I'd love to buy an Audi for my spouse
	x					I feel closer to another person when we go car shopping
						#3 Bargain Shopper
		x				I look for new car bargains whenever I can
		x				I always shop for the best new car value in town
						#4 Methodical Shopper
			x			I only shop for an Audi when I need a new car
			x			I go back to dealers who know how to treat customers well
			x			I don't like pushy car salespeople
						#5 Fun Oriented Shopper
				X		I wish buying a car was a lot more fun
				X		Auto shopping is stressful
						#6 Luxury Shopper
					x	I usually dress well when I go shopping at an Audi dealer
					x	Shopping for a car is a special experience
					x	I like car dealers who sell European designs

Table 13. Car Survey Segments

The Factor Analysis of the survey statements and answers has resulted in six segments reflecting group differences in consumer attitudes and perceptions. In this example, the segments provide insight into the different ways in which people approach buying new cars. When marketing to specific segments, such as segment #5, the promotional materials involved could promote car buying (and driving) as a "fun" experience. Alternatively, marketing to segment #2 could suggest messages about "love and relationships."

Using Predictive Modeling

Many firms also apply predictive models to their customer database to select individuals who will be mailed. For example, here are variables from one model that were used to predict automobile purchases:

Variable	Description	Type	Weight
Audi Owner	Existing Audi owner	+	23.1%
Recency	No months since last service	-	18.0%
Frequency	Total # service appointments	+	12.0%
Pres Club	Loyalty club towing member	+	13.0%
Gender	Male	+	7.0%
Gold Service	Opted in for Expanded service	+	7.0%
Pre-owned	Previously owned Audis	+	16.0%
Age	From 44-65	+	3.9%
			100%

Table 14. Examples of Variables Used in Predictive Modeling

In this case, the marketers used multiple regression equations to forecast future customer responses to promotions based on historical data (such as past purchasing behavior). All of the individuals on the database are scored according to the predictive model. The resulting scores are sorted, and the final mailing list is determined from the highest score down to the depth desired for the mailing.

In multiple regression models, the dependent variable (response) is determined by several independent variables (in this case, the characteristics and past behavior of the best customers). The weights are determined by the statistical program in terms of how much they explain or predict the dependent variable (e.g., response).

Once the regression model has been created, each individual is scored using their individual characteristics. For example, the automobile model determined the following scores for two of the individuals in the database: "124.1" and "minus 180.0." Since Inclusion in the mailing list is determined by the highest scores, the second customer would not be mailed.

Other variables, such as marital status, number of children, and type of vehicle owned, could be important predictors of future automobile purchases. If available, this data could be appended and used as part of an alternative scorecard or model. We can test several alternative predictive models to see which one produces a higher sales lift.

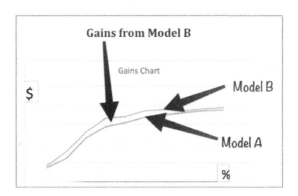

Figure 50. Gains Chart Comparing Predictive Models

Figure 50 shows the sales results based on the two alternative models. In this case, model B showed a sales gain, outperforming model A.

Another comparison showing sales for various models vs. a random sample of customers also helps to validate the performance of the model used to select recipients. The following gains chart shows that a considerable lift in sales was generated by using predictive models.

Figure 51. Gains Chart for Models Vs. Random Selection

The predictive model is more robust than RFM since it makes use of psychographic and demographic variables that RFM doesn't use. Moreover, RFM scores are usually included as part of the predictive regression equations. Thus, predictive modeling does take advantage of the RFM approach as well.

The predictive equations also allow us to determine the quality of the model's performance by seeing if there are differences between the actual and predicted sales results. Similarly, we can statistically measure how each variable (e.g., consumer characteristic, attitude, perception, etc.) has performed within the model in terms of predicting the consumer's response or purchase.

Summary

This chapter has addressed the importance of identifying our best customers as well as several approaches for accomplishing this.

The first of these approaches uses RFM, which offers both simplicity and explanatory power. In addition to selecting our best customers, RFM also gives us insights into the processes of attrition and migration.

Next, Factor Analysis is a key method used to segment customers on the basis of their attitudes and preferences. These dimensions are often more useful in predicting consumer purchasing behavior and can provide greater insight and power than demographics.

Finally, we reviewed the topic of Predictive Modeling by using regression equations to score an entire the database for the purpose of identifying our best customers. An additional lift in sales may be possible by creating and testing different models to see which model produces higher response rates and/or sales.

The next chapter presents the production process associated with direct mail marketing. Production will help us to understand the most efficient ways to prepare our customer files, as well as assure that our creative materials comply with government standards for entry and delivery via the postal system.

Action Steps

Looking at the customer RFM scores in Table 9, how would you describe and contrast the shopping behaviors of customers #540, #778 and #706. Which one of these would you consider the best customer? Why?

CHAPTER 6

GETTING A GRIP ON DIRECT MAIL PRODUCTION

Customer databases are messy places! Whether we maintain our customer files electronically, or on index cards in an office, we depend on them for email account information, customer addresses and phone numbers, and even customer names. Yet, many customer records in these files are simply not accurate and often contain false and misleading information. Even our purchased lists of names and contact information may contain serious flaws and errors.

Consider the amount of consumer information that we capture from sources such as social media sites, and at retail outlets and the like. The number of errors introduced into data systems at online points of sale or in retail stores, and via online chat rooms or other social media sites, is staggering. What kinds of errors are we talking about?

First of all, people don't always provide personal information. They may give false email addresses or phone numbers. Retail clerks may verbally capture information that hardly resembles what was said to them. And some employees just enter gibberish rather than taking the time to find the right fields or computer screens they need to enter customer data. All of these things compound a growing data problem. In addition to these woes, consider the rate in which databases tend to deteriorate. About 45 million people, or more than 10% of the United States population, move each year (Grumbine, 2018).

How many of these people still appear with old and outdated addresses on our customer databases? In addition, about 3 million people in the U.S. die each year as well (CDC, 2014). Unless we purge these names from our systems, we continue to mail and email them fruitlessly.

People also drop out and discontinue their commercial relationships. Suffice it to say, lost or inactive customer accounts may remain in our databases for years. All in all, the customer information in our database systems decays at a rate of approximately 25% (or ¼ of your total database listing) each year.

"Mission control, we have a problem," especially if we think that we can use all the information in our customer files, as we prepare to send out promotions for upcoming marketing campaigns. As we shall see, unless we routinely cleanse or hygiene our data files, we risk the integrity of what we currently have.

Data Hygiene

Let's look at some of the data quality problems that exist. Here is an excerpt from a company's recent mail file included for an upcoming direct marketing campaign:

Cust	First	Last	Address	City	State	Zip
160	, PO	KJHG	12KLHG	Sal	MA	01950
189	908	KLKJH	12KLHHG	NBV	MA	01950
218	,OPOi	KOIUJKH	27 Pleasant St.	NewberPort	MA	01950
433	Pete	Stahl 7391	103 Sherry Rd	Louisville	Ky	40217
436	<KB	Raj	1 Mill Street	Middleton	Ky	01949
568	LKL;JIO	MNVKJH	31 NKJH	San Jose	CA	95120

Table 15. Customer Data Errors

What we see is information that a sales associate entered incorrectly at the point of sale. In some cases, the associate entered or copied data into the wrong fields, presumably because the customer or company did not communicate well. Although these customers all made recent purchases, they cannot be identified nor contacted by mail in the future. The U.S. Postal System refers to these entries as "nixies," meaning that they are undeliverable as addressed and must by "nixed" or removed from the mail-stream.

Customer files often contain duplicate entries that are difficult to detect. For example, a name or address may contain enough differences to question whether they are variations for the same or for a different individual.

Here are some examples:

Cust ID	First	Last	Street	City	State	Zip
2003	Marilyn	Berman	100 Newberry Drive	Lawrence	MD	20706
3987	Manilyr	Burman	100 Newburg DR	Lawrence	MD	20706
1504	Erma	Williams	30 Carters LN	Riverdale	MD	20737
2111	Irma	Williams	300 Carrott Lane	Riverdale	MD	20737
2200	H	Williamson	45 East Street	Richville	MD	20721
7698	Hector	Wilson	45 E Street	Ritchville	MD	20721
2489	James	Rhoads	444 Ainer Road	Fort Washington	MD	20744
7783	James L	Rhodes	444 Amer Road	Ft Wash	MD	20744
4406	Jim	Roads	444 Amer Dr	Fort Washington	MD	20744
8891	Rita	Brothe	11 Ft Hills Circle	Mitchville	MD	20721
4663	Retta	Brodie	11 Ft Hills Drive	Mitchelville	MD	20721
2100	Rita	Brode	11 Ft Wash	Midville	MD	20721

Table 16. Customer Data Duplications

In some cases, we might suspect that despite the various duplicates, caused by misspellings or errors in the person's name, street address, or city, we are dealing with the same individual. However, it can be difficult to determine which entry is the correct version. This is a job for a service bureau that specializes in cleaning data by using proprietary algorithms which "dedupe" or remove duplicate records from data files (including name and address variations). The objective is to identify and leave the correct customer name along with their normal, standardized mailing address. Some of what they do, for instance, involves finding matching names based on sound, which would apply to the last name, "Rhoads, Rhodes, and Roads," in the example above. Additional processing would reveal which is the correct spelling and correct address.

To reduce the expense of mailing, it is economical to dedupe households down to one household member, as opposed to mailing everyone living in the household (e.g., householding). Here is an example of what the raw extract from the database might look like prior to the household cleansing:

Cust ID	First	Last	Address		State	Zip
7062	Stan	Schubert	258 West Pine Drive	Akron	OH	44321
3499	Susan	Schubert	258 W Pine Drive	Akron	OH	44321
2102	Dolores	Schubert	258 W Pine Road	Akron	OH	44321
5432	Jane	Schubert	258 West Pine Drive	Akron	OH	44321
1270	Peter	Schubert	258 West Pine	Akron	OH	44321
4331	Jane	Price	54 Havens Way Ct	Akron	OH	44333
7880	Joe	Price	54 Havens Way Ct	Akron	OH.	44333
2929	J	Price	54 Havens Way Ct	Akron	OH	44333
0115	Brian	Johnson	100 Merriweather Rd	Akron	OH	44333
6339	Darlene	Johnson	100 Merriweather Rd	Akron	OH	44333

Table 17. Customer Household Data Errors

The records above include multiple persons living at the same address. The deduping software used by the service bureau follows the client's instructions to determine which household member survives the purge. In this way, only one promotional piece is delivered to each address.

The cost savings from deduping and merge/purge cleansing can be enormous. Here is an example of the estimated savings calculated for a national mail-order catalog company:

Service	# Purged/Corrected	% Mailed	# Mailed	Savings
Dupes	400,000	25%	100K	$35,000
Nixies	300,000	25%	75K	$22,500
Addresses	700,000	25%	175K	$52,500
Total				$110,000

Table 18. Example of Data Hygiene Cost Savings

In this example, the data hygiene services would save the catalog company $110,000 by finding and purging duplicated records, and by correcting and standardizing undeliverable addresses. Many returned pieces can also be analyzed, and the client information updated to save those relationships.

Most printing houses today provide list management services aimed at correcting their clients' house files with updated customer information. In addition, the government also maintains lists of vendors or certified mail service providers (MSP's) that can help in complying with postal requirements to obtain lower postal rates.

In addition to private printing houses and service bureaus that specialize in data cleansing and mail handling, the Postal Service also offers an array of mail services that range from obtaining Mailer ID's to the printing of tray labels, sorting, coding and managing mail files that qualify for postage discounts. The online Business Customer Gateway and PostalPro area contain information as well as downloadable files for correcting and standardizing address information.

Let's take a look at some of the postal services that improve mailing list quality.

Using Address Correction Services

The data hygiene services which ultimately make mail handling more efficient and less costly overall include a series of programs provided by the United States Postal Service. Among the services provided are NCOA, MCOA, LACS, CASS and DSF2.

Most companies that use mass mailings use these services to make sure that their direct mailers comply with Postal Service rules and regulations. The benefits of doing so are three-fold: first, they can result in substantial postage rate discounts; secondly, they avoid penalties for non-compliance as well as avoiding mail delivery delays which could be catastrophic if one's mail is time sensitive. Thirdly, they increase response rates by standardizing and improving the accuracy of addresses so that the mail is delivered on-time to the targeted recipients. Finally, these services reduce the work of the post office, which in turn helps increase operating efficiency and reduces overall postal operating costs.

NCOA

The National Change of Address (NCOA) database is a product provided by the US Postal Service. NCOA compares a client's mailing list with some 160 million permanent address changes reported to the Postal Service within the last four years. Depending on how often one's files are updated, the NCOA services can update new addresses for individual, families or businesses who have moved within the last 18 to 48 months. These corrections can help companies realize up to a 15% distribution improvement by reducing the amount of undeliverable or delayed mail (US Postal Service, 2017).

Obtaining these updates is critically important for mass mailers. The USPS Move Update Requirement specifies that each mail file must be updated as to correct addresses within 95 days before the mailing date, with one of the USPS-approved methods. Over two billion mail pieces were returned or forwarded to senders in 2018, at an estimated cost to businesses of up to $25 per returned piece of mail (Pitney-Bowes, 2018).

Aside from avoiding penalties, the NCOA system provides one of the least expensive ways of obtaining new addresses for individuals who have moved. Mail can move through the system much faster, and more of it can reach its intended recipients.

MCOA

Although the NCOA service tracks individuals who have voluntarily given their change-of-address information to the post office, it does not capture movers who did not inform the Postal Service. This gap has been largely filled by MCOA (Multi-Source Change-Of-Address), a private service provided by Melissa Direct that lists some 120+ million records of people who have moved during the past 60 months (5 years). This database helps mailers stay up-to-date by capturing additional sources of customer migration. The new address information comes from a variety of sources that MCOA uses, e.g., magazine subscriptions, insurance companies, credit bureaus, mail order firms, etc. To obtain postage discounts, customer data records must be run hygiene at least twice a year.

LACS

Individuals who live in rural communities may not have addresses that can be used for mass mailings. For example, the listing of people in upstate New York might include such listings as Mr. Timothy Jones, Elk Creek Road, East Meredith, NY 13757 or Judith James, Turtle Top Farm, Bovina, New York, 13740. The LACS

(Locatable Address Conversion System) converts the rural listing to the address standards used in urban delivery areas. This information is also important for rural residents during fire or medical emergencies, since it helps community emergency response systems locate addresses more accurately and quickly.

DSF2

Mail delivery can be significantly improved if the location of the recipients is pinpointed as accurately as possible. The DSF2 (Delivery Sequence File, 2nd Generation) system sequences the order of mail piece delivery according to individual carrier routes. In addition, it corrects certain addresses by appending apartment numbers and suite numbers to mail pieces.

CASS™

The CASS certification (Coding Accuracy Support System) means that your mailing list has been validated for delivery with standardized addresses, including the accuracy of postal codes (5-digit zip codes, zip +4, and delivery point) on mail pieces. It allows for automation and bulk mail discounts as well as carrier route pre-sorts to facilitate mail delivery. CASS certification must be obtained 180 days prior to the mailing date (or 90 days for carrier route discounts).

AEC

AEC stands for the Address Element Correction System. It helps mailers correct problematic and incomplete addresses so that they can be delivered to the proper address.

ACS

The Address Correction Service is used in conjunction with Intelligent Barcodes to correct mailing labels and destinations.

DMACHOICE™

Members of the Data & Marketing Association (DMA) are required to adhere to consumer preferences about mail they do not wish to receive, such as credit offers, and catalog and magazine subscriptions. The consumer can opt out of these categories if they so choose. It is important that mailers suppress consumers in the mail file who do not want to receive a client's mail pieces.

Managing Mail Delivery

Most of the list services that have been described in this chapter involve software systems that improve the quality and accuracy of the addresses on the mailing list to make sure that the mail can be efficiently processed and delivered. The mail's appearance may also be changed physically, by adding barcodes and indicia, to speed up its delivery within the postal system.

INTELLIGENT MAIL BARCODES (IMB)

In general, all barcodes look impersonal and therefore translate into lower response rates. I'm not a great fan. Unfortunately, barcodes are both ubiquitous and inevitable, since they play a key role in terms of reducing cost, tracking mail, and accelerating mail delivery. We may choose to omit a barcode, only to have the USPS affix one anyway.

Aside from their aesthetic faults, barcodes usually carry a significant amount of information. Companies often add barcodes that are encoded with information about each customer that is used in post-campaign analysis. Postal Service barcodes carry information that is used to sort and track the mail from its origin to destinations (carrier routes).

John Q. Public
XYZ Company, Inc.
100 2nd Street
Anyplace, US 12345-6789

Intelligent Barcode

Figure 52. Example of Intelligent Bar Code

The USPS' Intelligent Barcode is used for domestic delivery and contains 65 bars of encoded information. This allows each piece to be traced to a point of delivery, so that organizations can analyze distribution and response patterns.

Tracking the mail through the postal system provides companies with a competitive advantage, particularly for time sensitive pieces related to upcoming sales events. To track the mail, pallets are seeded with coded samples of the mailing pieces, which are scanned at various distribution points throughout the postal system, and then reported online. Without tracking, the company is relying on wishful thinking that every piece will be delivered as planned. With tracking, the mail can be dropped closer to the sales events, since each real-time tracking scan shows if the delivery is on schedule.

The tracking system can alert a company when an unexpected problem occurs. Some years ago, for example, a major retailer realized that its mail to Pennsylvania customers was not being delivered for an upcoming sale weekend. The problem was immediately reported to the postal service, which determined that one truck loaded with the company's mail was missing. When postal inspectors found the truck and driver, he told them his car was being fixed, so he had used the truck to attend a family wedding! Although the sales flyers were late entering the system, they fortunately arrived on time.

QR™ Barcodes

QR™ barcodes also allow the marketer to track respondents and orders leading to improvements in future strategy.

QR Barcode
Scannable by smartphone

Figure 53. Example of QR™ Barcode

QR™ (Quick Read) barcodes are two dimensional barcodes, often seen on packaging and sales flyers. In direct marketing, they allow recipients to go directly to a web site, or landing site order page, without having to type in any information.

PALLETIZATION

Large volume mailers use palletization software in order to divide large quantities of mail into smaller amounts on pallets. Delivery to postal facilities is much easier when coding or processing individual pallets with smaller quantities (e.g., to make sure that the pallets are being delivered to the correct Bulk Mail Center or other distribution point). Palletization also helps secure optimal postal discounts since it improves Postal Service delivery and efficiency.

Mail from several companies may also be combined or comingled to obtain USPS discounts. The combined mail is sorted by zip code, tagged with intelligent bar codes, separated into trays according to zip codes, and trucked with all mail going to the same NDC or SCF destination (e.g., Network Distribution Center or Sectional Center Facility), where it is ultimately brought to a USPS post office, and delivered via individual carrier route to the customer's address.

Using Mail Lists

There are lists available by location for almost every conceivable interest, e.g., from lists of those who've recently divorced, to the newly engaged, and from individuals who like to climb mountains to those who prefer to fish for steelhead trout.

Most largescale printing firms can assist you in obtaining lists from brokers to reach specific target markets. In addition, such firms can also append data to company databases or mail files in order to enhance your existing customer lists with lifestyle data, including hobbies, such as gourmet cooking, horseback riding, and skiing, as well as political preferences, and community involvement, among other interests.

A quick search of Google reveals that there are many companies that sell mailing lists. Business.com published a report of the "Best Broker List Services" in 2018 in which they recommended several list companies, including InfoUSA, Mailing Lists Direct, and List Giant, to name a few (Business.com, 2018).

Some firms can compile their own Business to Business lists. A company offering computer training to local businesses, for example, should be able to build prospect lists from public sources such as phone and industry directories, as well as the online LinkedIn database, which provide key executive contact information including name, title, address, and telephone number. Obtaining prospective consumer lists, however, is usually not a do-it-yourself task. In the long run, the services of list brokers, printing firms, and direct mail agencies can provide access to demographic, psychographic, and lifestyle information that are compiled from various sources, such as magazine subscriptions, survey companies, public records, etc.

Multiple lists can also be used to identify some recipients. For example, in order to target wealthy prospects for investment management services, several lists were used in order to identify external signs of wealth, e.g., corporate position, casino credit holders, location of residence, airplane ownership, famous family name, etc.

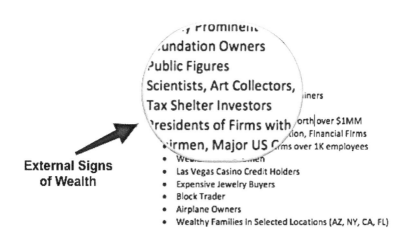

Figure 54. Use of Multiple Lists

The promotional materials were then mailed to individuals listed on a minimum of four lists. The most challenging part of the campaign were the follow-up telemarketing calls. These were essentially cold calls and were difficult to make for the executives who were asked to conduct the calls. Greater sales training and clarification of the telemarketing goals (e.g., secure meeting time and place) would have alleviated those problems.

Future mailings avoided these issues by changing the response mechanism so that the recipient requested a follow-up call or brochure. In this way, the recipient approved the calls in advance and there were no surprises when the contact calls were made. Overall, the firm was successful in adding several new investment clients through its direct marketing efforts.

Printing & Data Management Services

Direct mail marketing usually involves the printing and mailing of promotions to reach targeted audiences. Some organizations may opt to manage small mailings in-house and drop them at local postal facilities. However, when organizations reach out to larger quantities of customers, the need for automation discounts and more cost-effective methods of delivery becomes a key part of the overall mailing strategy. At this point, working with large capacity printers, who offer a range of data processing and printing services, becomes a necessity.

These services may include the following:

Data Processing
List Management
Data Hygiene
Postal Compliance & Optimization
Variable Data Printing & Inkjet Printing
Inserting & Finishing
Drop Shipping & Delivery Optimization
Comingling & Palletization

Figure 55. Mailing Services

Many printing firms also offer "omnichannel" or "integrated multichannel marketing" services, meaning that they also can provide email marketing and Social Media marketing assistance. In addition to executing the campaign, they can provide creative development for digital campaigns as well as conduct the analytics necessary to track and measure results.

Summary

This chapter has reviewed the challenges surrounding data quality and the need for data cleansing and hygiene. Various services, including NCOA, MCOA, LACS. SDF2 and CASS, provide a means to meet postal requirements, secure automation efficiencies, and improve mail accuracy and delivery. The physical mail must also meet postal requirements with respect to mail piece dimensions, and barcode label and stamp placement, as well as palletizing and pre-sorting for easier processing and delivery.

Working with Direct Marketing and Printing firms today is a necessity. These firms can process data files, design and print all promotional items, and prepare materials for entry into the postal system. Testing different printing vendors can help decide which one has better proprietary data hygiene software. Oftentimes, the cost of data hygiene alone more than compensates for the cost of these professional services.

Finally, working with Direct Marketing and Printing firms has an added benefit. Many of these firms also offer multichannel services. They can also aid in implementing, tracking and tabulating results for Email and Social Media marketing campaigns, which also happens to be the topic of our next chapter.

Action Steps

As you consider direct mail marketing, it is important to remember that working with a printing firm will make your life much easier. Such firms often handle smaller assignments as well as larger mass mailings. Do a quick search of the full-service direct marketing and/or printing firms in your area. Pick one that lists some services you may have an interest in and call them to ask if you can tour their facility.

Most companies like to demonstrate their printing capabilities as well as discuss the services they provide for their present clientele (including data hygiene, list management, etc.). In addition, many of these firms help their clients with online marketing services, and they can also provide detailed information about the costs and strategies for any upcoming campaigns you may be planning.

CHAPTER 7

CUSTOMER LIFETIME VALUE

Consider the following diagram:

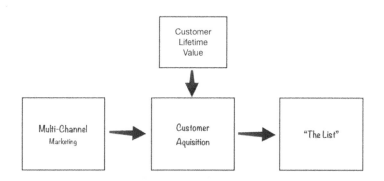

Figure 56. The Customer Acquisition Process

When it comes to growing one's business, companies often turn to Multi-Channel Marketing which includes direct mail marketing, as well as social media, email marketing, podcasts, and business blogging. Prospecting through these channels involves the same purpose: new customer acquisition. As we shall discover in this chapter, who marketers acquire and how they do so is largely determined by Customer Lifetime Value.

The goal of customer acquisition is the creation of the "List," which over time becomes a key company asset and determinant of an important company asset: customer equity or total customer value. The list of customers is usually maintained on the customer database, which contains all of the contact information, purchasing history, and characteristics about both existing and potential customers.

For new customers (who lack purchase histories and RFM scores), Customer Lifetime Value (CLV) provides a way of estimating their future revenue contribution to the company. Those with higher CLV's are our better customers who will spend more, while those with low CLV's are estimated as spending less over time.

Setting Acquisition Goals

One use of Customer Lifetime Value is to determine how many new customers we need to meet desired revenue goals. The following example demonstrates how an accounting company can use CLV to set its customer acquisition goals for its services to one of its customer segments, small businesses (sole proprietorships, small retail stores, etc.).

The company has defined Customer Lifetime Value (CLV) as the amount of revenue that the average customer produces over their estimated tenure with the company. In this case, the average price of the company's services to its small business clients is $5,000/year, the average customer tenure is 3 years, and the estimated Customer Lifetime Value equals $15,000, e.g., the amount the average customer will spend over a three-year period ($5,000 x 3).

	2018	2019	2020
Total Company Sales	2.2M	3.0M	5.0M
Small Business Revenue %	25%	27%	28%
Small Business Revenue	$300k	$800K	$1.4M
# New Customers	20	54	94

Table 19. New Customer Acquisition Goals

Note that the customer acquisition goals equal the projected small business revenues divided by the 3-year CLV. For 2018, the calculation would be $300K/$15K = 20). If the company wishes to reach its small business revenue goals, it must attract 20 new customers in 2018, 54 new customers in 2019 and 94 in 2020. The CLV is actually earned over a three-year period.

When we look at CLV this way, we notice some things that should concern us. First of all, we note that the company has ambitious goals for increasing its total revenue over the three-year period, e.g., from $2.2M in 2018 to $5.0M by 2020. In other words, the company intends to more than double its total revenue during this time frame. Although the percentage increase for the small business sector appears to be small, (from 25% to 28%), this amounts to a four-fold increase in small business revenue, and an almost five-fold increase in the number of new small business customers needed to meet this goal.

CLV allows us to consider different scenarios. If we can increase CLV, perhaps we can bring these numbers down to a more realistic acquisition level. Does the company know why clients in this segment leave after only three years? Perhaps the company's accounting fees are too high in comparison to its competition. The company may need to do some research to discover what other accounting firms are charging in its geographic area.

Another possibility is that small business clients are being somewhat neglected, while larger clients get the royal treatment. If small clients are profitable, then the accounting firm needs to consider making some managerial adjustments, perhaps assigning a senior partner to coordinate the services to their small business clientele. A survey of the small businesses could help detect if any service changes need to be made.

Let's assume that the company adds additional services to help its small business clientele, and that it now expects the small business tenure to increase to seven years. In that case, customer CLV increases also from $15,000 over three years to $35,000 over seven years (e.g., $5,000 x 7 = $35,000). How does this increase in CLV improve the customer acquisition numbers? Instead of needing 94 new customers by 2020, we now need only 40 ($1.4M/$35,000), hopefully a more doable and reachable number.

	2018	2019	2020
Total Company Sales	2.2M	3.0M	5.0M
Small Business Revenue %	25%	27%	28%
Small Business Revenue	$300k	$800K	$1.4M
# New Customers	9	23	40

Table 20. New Customer Acquisition Goals (Revision #1)

Since the company now provides more services to its small business clientele, let's also assume that the estimated annual revenue from the average client also increases from $5,000/year to $6,000/year, and that CLV over seven years, therefore, now increases to $42,000 (e.g., $6,000 x 7 = $42,000). As shown in Table 21, the number of new customers needed in order to generate the revenue goals is further decreased.

	2018	2019	2020
Total Company Sales	2.2M	3.0M	5.0M
Small Business Revenue %	25%	27%	28%
Small Business Revenue	$300k	$800K	$1.4M
# New Customers	7	19	33

Table 21. New Customer Acquisition Goals (Revision #2)

By noticing some problem areas and investigating how changing the CLV parameters could improve the situation, management is now in a good position to make changes that will help make these future projections a reality.

The accounting firm in this example was fortunate in that they knew the customer's CLV upfront, and they could use a simple CLV formula based on revenue. The revenue formula is easy to use and provides a quick look at alternative possibilities, so that management can consider different actions and plans. The simple revenue formula provides the company with several insights about acquisition, retention and churn (loss of customers).

Computing Customer Lifetime Value

However, the quick CLV approach may paint a picture that could be overly optimistic, since it ignores two factors. First of all, it ignores customer churn, the rate at which customers terminate their relationships, which tends to lower CLV. To account for the loss of customers each year, we use an estimated retention rate during future time periods.

Secondly, we are also dealing with future revenue and profits. Financial experts discount future dollar amounts by 1% to 10% to show that revenues earned in the future do not have the same value as revenue earned today (e.g., net present value). In addition, we often calculate CLV on profit rather than on revenue, a more conservative approach that factors in additional cost factors (Determann, 2015).

Equally important, many companies have no idea what their customers are worth to them, and they have never attempted to calculate their customers' lifetime value. CLV can be particularly enlightening for such companies. Once we know what a customer is worth (in terms of CLV), we can decide how much to spend on acquiring each new customer. We don't want to spend $100 to acquire a customer who is only worth $50 after three years. At the same time, we don't want to spend a mere $100 in acquisition costs when a customer has a CLV of $7500.

Consider, for example, that Starbuck's has calculated that their buyers have Customer Lifetime Values of $14,099 each (DesJardins, 2016). Is that coffee their selling or gold? How much should Starbucks spend in order to reach and attract each new customer?

A great advantage of CLV is that we can avoid a hasty assessment based on a brief view of new customers who may not, during the first year or so, appear particularly profitable. Since CLV represents revenue earned over a multi-year period, it may take several years before the profit earned for the average customer exceeds the customer's acquisition costs. For example, consider the following CLV calculation in Table 22 for a Colorado based guitar manufacturer (which introduces a scenario adjusted for customer retention rates, profit, and discounted cash value):

	Year 1	Year 2	Year 3
# Customers	10,000	5,000	3,500
Retention Rate	50%	70%	75%
Order /Year	3.0	4.0	5.0
Average Order Size	$150	$175	$200
Total Revenue	$4.500,000	$3,500,000	$3,500,000

Cost Margin	65%	60%	55%
Cost of Goods Sold	$2,925,000	$2,100,000	$1,925,000
Sales Costs per Customer	$175	$150	$100
Sales Costs	$1,750,000	$750,000	$350,000
Total Costs	$4,675,000	$2,850,000	$2,275,000

Gross Profit	($175,000)	$650,000	$1,225,000
Discount Rate*	1	1.16	1.35
Net Present Value (NPV)*	($175,000)	$560,345	$907,407
Cumulative NPV Profit	($175,000)	$385,345	$1,292,752
Customer Lifetime Value	($17.50)	$38.53	$129,28

*Net Present Value is the value of money to be received in the future using a discount rate (often from 1% - 10%)

Table 22. Customer Lifetime Value (Three-Year Period)

Without CLV, it would look like the acquisition of new customers was not profitable during the first year. Indeed, some businesses (which do not use CLV) may panic if they see negative numbers initially, not realizing that the first-year loss of $175,000 is only temporary. There is a profit of $385,345 in Year 2, and $1.2 million by Year 3. In haste, management may call for a number of changes in performance that really aren't needed.

When we use CLV, a much larger and accurate perspective is gained. The average CLV for the three years is $50.10 (-$17.50+$38.53 +$129.28/3). This also suggests that we would not want to exceed this amount in acquisition spending on a per customer basis. In this way, the CLV calculation can act as a guide to our marketing or sales budgets, as well as give us a more realistic view of the company's economic health.

In many cases, we want to drill down to the individual customer level to see what the CLV is for each customer. Here's one example of customers for a furniture retailer. To account for the loss of customers each year, we use an estimated retention rate during future time periods.

High Value Customers

Cust ID	Av. Sale $	# Sales Yr.	$Sales Yr.	Estimated Retention (Years)	Total Sales	Av. Cost of Goods Sold $	Profit Margin $	CLV
2349	150	2	300	3	900	115	23.33	$209.97
0002	300	1	300	5	1500	250	16.67	$349.80
1220	175	3	525	5	2625	125	28.57	$749.96
3546	600	4	2400	8	19.200	525	12.50	2400.00
1700	375	2	750	5	3750	295	21.33	799.88

CLV = Av Sale x Sales. Year x Retention x Profit Margin; Av Sale = Total Sales / # Sales Year; Profit Margin = (Av Sale − Av COGS)/Av Sale x 100

Table 23. Customer Lifetime Value for Individual Customers

Similar to RFM, we can categorize customers into various segments by using Customer Lifetime Value. In this case, we can identify the High Value Customers with CLV's of $700+), the Medium Value customer having a CLV's from $300 to $699, and the Low Value customer in the top row having CLV's below $300. Most of our marketing strategy would focus on catering to the High Value segment of customers, such as customers #1220, #3546 and #1700 in Table 23.

Direct Marketing

Consider this situation: A Customer Lifetime Value of $150 is an estimate of what a customer will spend over a course of one or more years. When you send out a direct marketing campaign and

$150 CLV customers respond, it's important to remember that a $50 initial purchase during the campaign may not be profitable due to the direct marketing costs involved. It's the $150 that the CLV customers are going to spend over the course of their relationship with the company that creates the desired amount of profits.

Mailed	Cost	Response %	Price	# Orders	Profit /Loss	CLV $150 Over 3 Yrs.
10K	$5k	1.0%	$25	100	($2,500)	$10,000
25K	$15k	1.2%	$25	300	($7,500)	$30,000
45K	$25K	1.5%	$25	675	($8,125)	$76,250

Table 24. Direct Marketing Profitability (CLV = $150/ 3 Yrs.)

In this example, we first see the result of three waves of mailings, which produced orders of 100 units, 300 units and 675 units, at a price of $25. Without CLV in the picture, the focus would be on the Profit/Loss generated by this campaign in the first year, and the resulting losses each wave produced. This, however, is a distorted picture.

With an understanding of Customer Lifetime Value, we see that each mailing produced responses of customers who have a CLV of $150 over 3 years. Thus, the first wave produced 100 respondents who would each spend $150 over the next 3-year period, or $15,000. Since the first wave mailing cost $5,000, the company would see a net profit over three years of $10,000. In other words, they invested $5,000 in the mailing in order to earn $10,000, a return of 100%.

In the second wave, they spent $15,000 and received orders from 300 respondents who would also spend $150 over three years, or $45,000 in total. Deducting the $15,000 for the mailing (as an acquisition cost essentially), leaves the company with a profit of $30,000, as shown in the last column. The company doubled its investment, not a shabby return.

Finally, in the third mailing wave, the company received orders from 675 individuals with CLV's of $150. Over the next three years, this group will spend $101,250. Deducting the mailing (or acquisition) costs of $25,000, leaves a profit to the company over a three-year period of $76,250. That's a 3X return on the investment.

Knowing the Customer Lifetime Value certainly puts things into perspective. CLV is an important number to marketers. Without it, we would not see the anticipated revenue that new customers represent over time.

One thing that marketers quickly realize is that they can earn more profits by increasing a customer's CLV. You can do so by using your customer database strategically and targeting each group of consumers with the products and services that they value most, as well as rewarding them with special sales events and prices that celebrate their loyalty status.

If the company has communicated effectively and provided superior service to its customers, the result usually is additional upselling opportunities to more expensive products, and more cross-selling to other product lines of interest. Over time, the CLV would also rise. Let's say that the CLV for three years now amounts to $225 per average customer rather than $150 in the example above.

What would be the impact on direct mail profit? We'll keep everything else the same in the following chart, except for CLV, which increases from$150 to $225.

# Mailed	Cost	Response %	Price	# Orders	Profit/Loss	CLV $225 Projected Over 3 Years
10K	$5k	1.0%	$25	100	($2,500)	$17,500
25K	$15k	1.2%	$25	300	($7,500)	$52,500
45K	$25K	1.5%	$25	675	($8,125)	$126,875

Table 25. Direct Marketing Profitability (CLV = $225/3 Yrs.)

By taking CLV into account, we see that the marketing campaign is more profitable when CLV increases from $150 to $225. In effect, the company has attracted 1075 new customers from the entire mailing, each having a CLV of $225, and an earnings potential in total of $241,875 (an increase in spending potential over three years of $80,625 compared to a CLV of $150).

The calculation of CLV does vary from company to company, as there is no standard or agreed upon formula. In fact, there are at least six or seven CLV versions that exist online, and some use different parameters (such as the number of new customer referrals suggested by existing customers). The good news is that there are a number of online CLV calculators available, as well as downloadable Excel CLV spreadsheets. Therefore, calculating CLV has been largely automated and does not have to be done manually.

Finding a CLV approach that suits each company should not be a difficult task. The company should choose a particular CLV formula and adhere to its calculations consistently. CLV should prove to be an extremely useful measure of customer value while improving a number of marketing and financial decisions.

Summary

Customer lifetime value provides us with a way to quantify how much a customer is worth to us, whether that customer is a new respondent to a direct mail or email promotion or is an online subscriber to social media. CLV guides us in determining new customer acquisition goals and budgets. In addition, we can use CLV on an individual customer level to segment our database and customer lists into high value, medium value and low value customers to target customers with the greatest sales potential.

Without the benefit of CLV, managements could easily misinterpret the results of their marketing efforts. CLV provides a means of projecting revenue and profit sources into the future, based on existing customer spending and retention rates. Oftentimes, these are parameters that need improvement too. Our objective is to increase CLV for customers by providing exceptional service and products.

The timing of offers, and persistent engagement with customers is crucial today to establish and maintain an online and offline brand presence.

Action Steps

If your company or organization doesn't use Customer Lifetime Value currently, how would you approach management to persuade them to consider developing a test in this area? If they put you in charge of a trial project, what steps would you take?

CHAPTER 8

MULTICHANNEL MARKETING

Although this book is about direct mail marketing, we have many reasons to encourage the use of digital channels, which have grown exponentially. When multichannel consumers shop across channels, their response rates increase significantly on *all* channels. Customers who shop across multiple channels also become more valuable to us. Their average purchase size and overall lifetime values also increase significantly, and the retention of the best customers also improves. What happens online, therefore, continues to affect direct mail results offline to an ever-increasing degree.

Customers who shop across multiple channels have one thing in common: higher response rates. Direct mail marketers can reap the benefits from online relationships by learning how to reach out to their customers via emails, social media, podcasts and blogs. By interacting online with consumers, we improve our brand presence, as well as our ability to offer products and services that have greater relevance to our customers' current and future needs.

Multichannel marketing recognizes the importance of all channels and online platforms that affect our companies and customers. Multichannel platforms have differences in how they operate and what subscribers can and cannot do. These differences ultimately affect the nature of the customers' interactions and how we market to them.

Email and social media, for example, have their own sets of standards, as well as best practices. For example, organizations should avoid promotions that could be construed to be "junk emails" or spam. Individual social media sites (e.g., Facebook, Twitter, Instagram, LinkedIn, Pinterest, YouTube, Snapchat, and Flickr) have their own guidelines and prohibitions about the nature of subscriber contact, largely based on broadcast quantity and content.

Social media encompasses what we formerly called "word-of-mouth." Ironically, word-of-mouth no longer occurs face-to-face, but via computer-to-computer. Marketers have always dreamed about harnessing the power of word-of-mouth, as an extension of their advertising efforts. The idea was to influence consumers positively, so that they, in turn, would spread the word about our products and brands to others.

Social media has given us a new connection to the advertising audience. The challenge now is to adapt our marketing strategies to the digital environment to create and sustain a community interested in our brands that leads to greater loyalty and higher sales.

We have the opportunity to interact with many consumers simultaneously, and to customize experiences for each consumer for a truly one-on-one experience. Such activities have the potential for creating and sustaining favorable impressions over time. Every consumer who has a positive experience now becomes a potential ambassador for our brand. Through this constant real-time vigilance and creativity, social media will allow the formation of brand loyalties that can be individualized, are considerably stronger, and go much deeper emotionally than ever before.

Customer complains on
Facebook about store issue

Customer Service
reponds immediately

Figure 57. Customer Service Online Intervention

Having a commercial brand presence on social media sites, such as Facebook, is no longer just an option. Whether you like it or not, you are now part of an online community, where people can comment and express their opinions on almost anything, including your brand, as well as vent their disappointments and concerns.

It's amazing, for example, how we take for granted the ability of companies to intervene immediately to correct a consumer's problem. Most companies do well in monitoring their Facebook accounts, so that any negative posted comments are dealt with instantaneously, which often leaves their customers feeling satisfied and often surprised as well. Customer service earns high marks for the exchange shown above.

Social Media Platforms

How should you begin your marketing journey into Social Media?

Some experts suggest that you should start with a Digital Marketing Plan, as well as your goals, projected sales, and your online marketing strategy. However, before any sort of marketing plan can be done, it's important that you begin by immersing yourself in social media sites. If you are going to be successful in marketing to social media users, you first need to identify: who the social media users are, where they are, and what they are doing there. Since many of these consumers shop offline, these insights will inevitably improve our direct mail marketing efforts as well.

Trying to conduct reconnaissance on each social platform can be an exhausting experience, even if you limit your scope to the major sites, such as Facebook, LinkedIn, Twitter, Instagram, YouTube, and Pinterest. Thankfully, there are a number of Social Media Management Applications that can automate your presence and experience across several sites. These include Hootsuite, Buffer, TweetDeck, SocialOomph, IFTTT, SpredFast, SocialFlow, Sprout Social, Everypost, and Tailwind. We will review one or two of these tools in this chapter.

Each of the social media management tools provides a dashboard that automates access to your social media accounts and allows you to interact across networks and avoid the need for manual postings on individual sites.

In essence, these applications provide you with a command center which simplifies the task of scheduling posts on multiple sites, such as Facebook, LinkedIn, Twitter, etc.

With Hootsuite, perhaps the most popular social media management system, you can interact with others at any time as well as monitor and filter social conversations by keyword (in multiple languages) to track attitudes about your company and your competition. And if you are managing a commercial business online,

Interact when
mentioned, etc.

Go to Facebook, Twitter,
LinkedIN etc. to see activity,
schedule comments, etc.

HOOTSUITE DASHBOARD

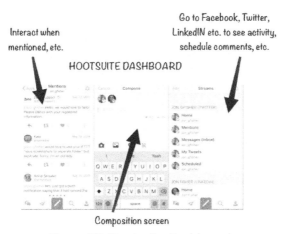

Composition screen

Figure 58. Hootsuite Dashboard

you can use Hootsuite's analytics, allowing you to monitor Key
Performance indicators (KPI's) including ROI, for each of your online
accounts. You can also access your social media accounts via
desktop or mobile phone.

The following screenshot shows an example of Hootsuite's
automatic scheduling screen which allows you to add hundreds of
social media posts across your accounts at times you specify
(perhaps as part of next weekend's sales campaign).

Auto schedule Text Message

Add Images

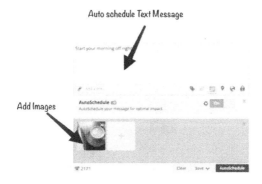

Figure 59. Hootsuite Automatic Text Scheduling

One of the social media management systems, called Thryv, has positioned itself as an all-in-one software for "small businesses," and it too comes with a suite of online tools and monitoring procedures. The Thryv social media management system is currently used by over 50,000 small businesses with access to an array of services that help manage online strategy, including:

- Customer Relationship Management (with "insights" about their customers and contact)

- Communications (texts and emails including automated messaging and follow-ups)

- Advertising (advertising placement and optimization)

- Online Presence (on 60+ top listing sites)

- Appointments and Bookings (calendar and online scheduling)

- Social Media Engagement (social postings and promotions, instant responses to ratings and reviews, personalized library of posts, and newsfeed timing)

- Payments (quotes, invoices, and payment processing)

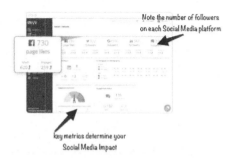

Figure 60. thryv Dashboard

While some service providers take a broad-brush approach to an online presence, a number of popular social media management providers cater to just one site. TweetDeck, which was acquired by Twitter, is a free application that focuses solely on Twitter, allowing users to manage an unlimited number of Tweeter accounts at the same time. Working within a browser, the TweetDeck interface can initiate tweets, retweets, replies, and it also organizes Twitter lists, searches, notifications, and hashtags.

Similarly limiting itself to one area, Hashtag Expert is a hashtag App for Instagram. Starting with one's own topics of interest or base hashtags, the App recommends similar ones that can be copied and posted. The App can save hashtag groups, reuse them, and view the most popular hashtags in a Trending section. In addition, the App provides an assessment of how well a hashtag group will perform by issuing a Hashtag Report Card. Hashtags can also be viewed by category or by niche.

In a similar vein, some social media companies focus on specific online functions. Alliance Sweepstakes, an online promotional marketing company, concentrates all of its efforts on assisting companies in managing online contests, sweepstakes, and game promotions to clients around the world.

Contests, games and sweepstakes may help build positive brand feelings within the online community. Imagine the excitement that is created when you launch a contest to win tickets to a championship football game!

A Chance to Win Tickets to A Football Championship!

Figure 61. Example of Online Contests

Here's a secret: the best contests are those where everyone is a winner! That is, no one is a loser when every person receives something, even if it is only a keyring for their favorite team. It's a good idea to research your customer base and make sure that contests will be well received and provide the desired results.

Alliance, another management platform, provides help with strategies, platforms, and games, including

- Legal consultation and guidance

- Social media integration and site compliance

- Surety bonds and state registrations

- Procurement of affidavits and liability releases

- Prize selection, procurement, fulfillment & taxation

Alliance's objective is to deliver a "worry-free" promotion that "minimizes risk and maximizes results." Given the particular subject area, these services should provide considerable peace of mind.

Another management service, AgoraPulse, monitors the three most popular social media platforms, Facebook, Twitter and Instagram. AgoraPulse offers a full range of services, including a "Barometer" dashboard to gauge site performance in comparison to competitor's websites (companies seeking the same subscribers). The ability to

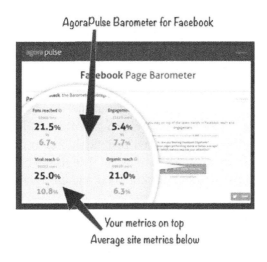

Figure 62. Comparing Metrics & Competitive Benchmarks

see what competitors are achieving provides important insights that can lead to changes in present and future strategies.

Agorapulse allows users to track and respond to posts and comments and as well as spot brand and keyword mentions, which can then be tagged for more in-depth analysis. Business.com (2019) suggests that this feature makes it easy to identify and interact with key followers and influencers, and particularly those individuals whose word-of-mouth activities increase your brand's awareness and sales.

Virtually all the social media management platforms offer some degree of automation, usually with respect to the scheduling of emails, posts, comments, and replies. Tailor Social, a social media management platform, focuses its efforts on content, providing a solution to the problem that many users undoubtedly experience, e.g., what to publish on your social channels. The Tailor Social system makes content suggestions based on the engagement with subscribers, as well as "relevancy and freshness." You begin by selecting Topic Categories, followed by Keywords for each topic, and ultimately choose among suggestions of "stimulating" visuals and content.

With the help of a Design Feature, the user chooses images, backgrounds, and texts to enhance messages as measured by shares, likes and comments. Throughout this process, the Tailor Social platform makes suggestions about content, while the user also has the option of adding their own additional commentary, images, blog content, videos, and news. The user's posts can be published using an automated scheduler and calendar.

These social media management platforms are representative of what is available online for organizations that want to engage with their online clientele. Overall, they provide a user interface or dashboard for either interacting with individual clients, or simultaneously with large numbers of social media subscribers. The platforms include tools for analytics, creative design, and scheduling that allow smaller businesses to compete successfully against much larger firms.

Digital Advertising Strategy

There are two general content planning guidelines for determining the best ways to advertise online. Rule 4-1-1 was developed by Tippingpoint Labs as a recommendation for Twitter users that has become generic and widely used across all kinds of social media sites (Bigfoot Digital).

According to Rule 4-1-1, online consumers became annoyed by uninvited and intrusive messages, and they become disenchanted with the brands involved. What the 4-1-1 Rule suggests is that out of every six social media posts, businesses should make sure that four of them avoid any kind of hard self-promotion. Instead, one's posts should reflect entertaining, newsworthy or interesting content. As a general guideline, the four posts should be relevant to the consumer's needs and geared towards subjects such as education, entertainment, and current news.

One of the six posts can be a "soft" promotion, such as an interesting story, event, shared or ungated content (e.g., freely available for download) that is tied specifically to the sponsored product or service. A soft sell approach is a subtle form of persuasion using a more gentle, low pressured approach. The soft sell helps establish us as a source of meaningful information and dialogue in order to build online rapport and trust.

The soft sell message can also reinforce the company's direct mail marketing materials and promotional campaigns being conducted offline. According to M. De Veirmann, soft advertising does this because it is "perceived as less irritating, and more credible," and leads to a "higher intention to share, due to the generation of positive attitudes towards the ad" (De Veirmann, 2015). In short, soft advertising tends to create positive ties between a company and its prospects, as a means of developing a long- term relationship and sales.

The sixth post, can be a "hard" or self-serving promotion along with a related call-to-action, including a request for additional information, completion of an order form, or sweepstakes entry to win a prize, etc.

Sabrina Pack suggests that the 4-1-1 rule ensures that the content of a company's social media posts will be varied and that they will be fresh and stimulating "and not rooted in endless repetition of the same subject" (Pack, 2017). Essentially, the 4-1-1 rule supports online brand building, a criterion for effective online promotions and advertising.

The second content rule, the 70-20-10 Rule, is another useful guideline for posting materials online. In this case, Rule 70-20-10 suggests that 70% of a company's posts should bring value to the community, including relevant ideas, events, and survey results. About 20% of the online posts can be about another local or outside source. For example, LinkedIN members often share interesting articles that other members have written. The remaining 10 percent of posts can be promotional or sales oriented, or even a recommendation of another product or brand, that the audience might appreciate hearing about.

These rules can also be used as guidelines for advertising in social media space as well as the internet space in general. The important point is that the sponsoring company/brand or logo must be clearly identified and associated with any soft sell promotion.

Of course, all online advertising must reach interested consumers. Tanner Larsson, ecommerce entrepreneur and consultant, reiterates that all advertisements must be targeted to online consumers based on their passions and interests with pertinent affinity and brand loyalties, such as, cooking (e.g., Betty Crocker), autos (e.g., Tesla Model 3), and fashion (e.g., Ralph Lauren) (see Larsson, 2010, 2016).

Email Marketing

Hootsuite's publication, *A Simple Formula for Converting Facebook Traffic into Sales*, applies a modified 4-1-1 Rule to Email Marketing on Facebook as a means of increasing conversion rates. Hootsuite notes that "emails can tell a bigger story than a single Facebook ad, particularly for a complex or expensive product" (Hootsuite.com).

The reason Hootsuite picks Facebook as the target site is simple: 2 billion people use Facebook every day. Hootsuite suggests sending out the following series of emails:

Step One: Bonus Email – An offer of free information (industry Report, discount, etc.,) in exchange for the prospect's Email address. The same offer appears in a Facebook Lead ad.

Step Two: A funny or interesting story focusing on the use of your product
Step Three: Explain how your product solves a problem for consumers

Step Four: A funny personal story about how you discovered the product o started the company.

Step Five: Your product offer with testimonials, other reassurance measures.

Step Six: Repeat formula again with similar offers.

Table 26. Email Marketing & The 4-1-1 Rule

Not only do 98.4% of all consumers check their email each day, they do so multiple times! (Privy Academy, 2017). Email platforms improve the accuracy of email addresses, and therefore the likelihood of hitting their mailboxes and being acted upon.

Email Marketing Platforms

There are many email marketing platforms that address the use of emails online. They include Mailchimp, Infusionsoft, SendGrid, GetResponse, Constant Contact, and others. Most of these solutions address the two major concerns users may have: how do I acquire email lists of prospects, and how do I use emails to convert them to customers?

According to Wpbeginner.com, three things must be in place to build an email list: a website or blog, an email marketing service, and user-friendly opt-in forms. All email lists begin with an opt-in. You attract people to your website or blog, and cordially invite them to give you their email address in exchange for something of value (wpbeginner.com). The opt-in page may be a pop-up that may look something like this:

Figure 63. Customer Opt-In Page

By opting in, the customer has self-selected to become a part of your email list. With this list, you can send private messages to each person and target them with offers for which they have been pre-qualified. Because you know already their interests and affiliations, your email conversions may reach 10X that of social media sites! (wpbeginner.com).

Although marketers buy lists of prospects for direct mail marketing, buying a list for email marketing is generally not recommended due to the expense, uncertain quality and generally poor results (optinmonster.com). By choosing one of the email management platforms, you can gain traction by building your own lists of customers belonging to various online interest groups and communities. We will review three email platforms here.

The Constant Contact platform offers a variety of services that are useful for interacting effectively with email subscribers, including automated personalized welcome messages, birthday acknowledgments, and anniversary templates. Prospects click on specific advertising content, so that the more relevant emails can be targeted to them and better results are obtained. The site's segmentation tools also identify and group together like contacts or prospects, thus spreading the "fishing net" out further.

In addition, emails can be uploaded from email messaging tools (such as Gmail, Outlook, etc.), and added to your email lists and scheduled campaigns. Updates are automatically made for bounces, inactivity, and unsubscribers. The service also makes suggestions concerning content, images, and captions, and it also provides analytics and tracking of individuals who open and share your emails and social posts.

Infusionsoft is another well-known platform that supports small businesses with email management services designed to optimize customer relationships, lead capture, and e-commerce. With a considerable amount of "how to" training content, Infusionsoft's user blog aids users with numerous tips and suggestions. These include how to craft authentic subject lines, build action buttons, ask visitors to share content, use preheader texts, and time email delivery to the time of day when such messages are normally read.

The suggestion to use pre-header texts is an interesting one. Preheaders are summary texts that follow the subject line when the email is viewed in the inbox. It is used by recipients to pre-screen an email's contents before the email is actually opened.

The fragment of a preheader text that appears in the preview box is often overlooked by most email senders. Optimizing this with something that is thought-provoking or that evokes curiosity can significantly improve opening rates.

Figure 64. Preheader Optimization

With Infusionsoft, emails can be dropped into different sales funnels or pages with different text messages for upselling, webinar enrollment, and free pdf file downloads to build email lists. In addition, the software can facilitate setting appointment dates or direct visitors to an affiliate's page for sales by related networks. The range of sales funnels helps to enhance email tracking and as well as interactions with prospects.

Another email platform, ClickFunnel, is also geared towards marketing to email lists, and supports a large variety of sales-oriented pages. What sets ClickFunnels apart is its intuitive, drag-and-drop user interface. Elements such as landing page headlines and images can be dragged into place. Webinar pages, appointment reminders, and videos can be easily added to landing pages and configured to autoplay when an individual reaches the page. ClickFunnel has also included some key features, such as an "add-to-cart" button as well as a built-in sales processing feature, so that a landing page can turn into a full-fledged ecommerce site.

Active Campaign, our last email management platform, excels with its automation capability. When someone subscribes to a list, you create several automated contact funnels. You can monitor email subscribers via tags to see how many open emails, click on links, or take other actions. You can tag subscribers to visit your website or Facebook group, change subscribers from one group to another, alter email delivery times, or schedule a drip campaign (e.g., sending a series of emails coinciding with subscriber actions). Active Campaign comes with a Preheader text editor too, and it also integrates with over 150 plug-in apps including WordPress, Zapier, Shopify and Clickfunnels (to capture email addresses).

There are many more email management platforms available on the internet. Many can be used for a free trial period at little or no cost or have different levels of use that cost more as one adds services. For example, the lowest user level of Active Campaign costs just $17/month. If you intend to use an email campaign manager (and why wouldn't you?), just Google additional email platform possibilities, or check out the ones mentioned in this book.

"To Blog or Not to Blog, That is the Question"
(with apologies to William Shakespeare and Hamlet)

The answer to the question above is decidedly YES, all businesses need to blog!

Blogging has come a long way, particularly Business blogging! In fact, it has now become a business necessity, and any business that hasn't caught on to this yet needs to look into it asap.

Business blogging accomplishes many positive things for a business: in particular, it creates more online visibility and helps drive traffic to your website. In an article published on hubspot.com, Corey Wainwright explains that every blog is another indexed page on your website, making your website that much more visible and easier to search and find. "Blogging is a marketing channel (just like social media, direct mail, email marketing, etc.) that helps support business growth" (Wainwright, 2015).

Business blogging supports business activities by creating visibility and interest. According to Wainwright, the content of blog posts can enhance a company's presence and authority on the internet by

- Providing new and interesting content for sharing by social media users
- Increasing web traffic via calls-to-action
- Increasing consumer satisfaction with offers of free trials, offers, etc.
- Generating interest and visits in future months and years (Wainwright, 2015).

It's important to note that blogging is a long-term commitment. Your existing and potential clientele will start to look forward to reading your blogs, and they will not react well if you feel that it's just too much work and you decide to discontinue it. Abrupt cancellations of blogs have the potential for alienating customers and/or creating animosity.

Blogs are similar in content to podcasts, although blogs are designed for reading on computers, while podcasts are auditory and designed for listening via iPod, MP3 player, Apps, cell phones, etc. Approximately, 1/3 of the US population aged 12-24 listen to podcasts each month; while only 13% of adults aged 55 and over listen monthly. Podcasts reach younger markets, e.g., millennials, Generation Y and Generation Next (Baer, 2018).

Blogging Platforms

There are a host of blog platforms from which to choose that can help to facilitate the process. These include Wordpress, Joomla, WIX, Blogger, Weebly, Ghost, Tumblr, Squarespace, and Medium, to name a few. Most blog platforms are easy to use, can be tailored to the focus or subject you want, and provide flexibility for adding additional services as you grow. We'll review a few examples here to show the type of support that they provide.

Blogs function pretty much the same way as a website, although the emphasis on the blog is on the publication of information, ideas, opinions, news flashes, and other humorous, pithy and captivating content. In addition, blogs now contain calls for action such as order forms and such, which sounds very much like the ecommerce activity that you would find on most commercial websites today.

The purpose of the business blog is to keep consumers interested in the company's products and presence online. An article by Katherine Keller suggests that "Google has helped take the work out of networking by connecting potential customers to potential business owners twenty-four hours a day, seven days a week" (Keller, 2017). This change in the business model means that businesses must become proficient in these skills in order to upgrade their arsenal of marketing tools.

Wordpress.com is the premier host for websites and blogs. It provides a cornucopia of designs and themes, allowing users to create a free website with a significant amount of storage. Optional plans with more advanced features, such as domain name selection and registration, ecommerce tools, and a vast array of plugins and advanced support are also available. With Wordpress, users can create websites and blogs, embed audio and videos, drag-and-drop images into posts and pages, access Wordpress' editors that include HTML, and access site statistic reports, along with basic search engine optimization tools. The basic blog or website starts out Free for life, but users undoubtedly add on more advanced features and services as soon as they can.

As it says on their website, Wordpress accounts for about "31% of the Internet." With a 55% market share, Wordpress powers many websites and blogs of major companies, including the New York

Times, CNN, Forbes, Reuters, General Motors, United Parcel Service, SONY, Best Buy, eBAY, among others (websitesSetup.com). In contrast, Joomla has a 20 % market share, while Drupal's has a 11% market share (Internetlivestats.com). Robert Mening, a blogging advocate, has noted that all three management platforms give users an ability to maintain a first-class presence on the Internet (Mening, 2019).

Joomla was originally introduced in 2005 and it has evolved into a relatively easy-to-use digital content management systems (CMS) platform. Joomla is free and is an open-sourced CMS service that is non-corporate sponsored and managed by its own community of users. It provides search engine optimization and it is accessible by mobile users. Having won many awards, Joomla markets its platform as being completely customizable, noting that users can access thousands of graphic user interfaces (gui's) and text templates (many for free) as well as third party applications. Joomla is supported by an extensive amount of documentation, including video training. In addition, there is an active Joomla community forum which links users from around the world.

Drupal was founded in 2001 and ranks third among website and blog CMS platforms. Drupal notes that it is the #1 platform for web management among global enterprises, governments, universities and NGO's (non-government community organizations). It is supported in multiple languages, and is also a free, community-based system. Drupal is a highly scalable and flexible system that can accommodate high traffic situations, as is evidenced by such Drupal user sites such as Weather.com, Grammy.com and Time, Inc. (Drupal.com). It is also supported by a worldwide Drupal community of users.

Summary

This chapter has addressed the importance of multichannel marketing, which includes Direct Mail Marketing, Social Media,

Email Marketing, and Blogs and how they support one other by engaging the consumer online and offline.

It is incumbent upon marketers to create an effective online brand presence, as well as establish a lasting dialogue with consumers. The goal is to engage prospective customers, and to build relationships that are interactive and ongoing. Social media allows us to establish links with customers that would be impossible anywhere else.

This chapter has reviewed a number of Social Media Management Applications, such as Hootsuite, Thryv, Hashtag Expert for Instagram, Alliance Sweepstakes, and Agorapulse. Each of these platforms enhances the way in which we interact with our customers.

We've also looked at Rule 4-1-1 and Rule 70-20-10 which are used as guides with respect to how we implement digital advertising and email contact strategies. In addition, we considered the use of email marketing platforms, such as Infusionsoft, Constant Contact, Clickfunnel, and Active Campaign. The topic of preheaders was also discussed as one key strategy for increasing email opening rates.

Finally, we considered the use of business blogs, and how these may contribute to a company's online image and presence. The three largest blog platforms, Wordpress, Joomla and Drupal, were briefly reviewed.

Today, we can no longer afford to work in isolated silos of marketing activity. We now have an arsenal of effective online marketing tools that never existed until today's technology made them possible.

Offline marketing efforts, such as direct mail marketing, continue to provide high response rates and revenue streams. This area of marketing is also supported by new and advanced technological systems. It's important to remember that each marketing channel offers its own unique advantages as well as opportunities to engage customers more profitably and effectively than ever before.

Action Steps

As noted above, business blogs have become an important part of the online presence of many companies. Those blogs ordinarily publish a variety of stories and anecdotes relating to their products and services. Pick one or two of your favorite companies. If the company is in retailing, stop by one of its stores and ask any of the personnel if they can tell you about the company's business blog. You may get a lot of blank stares. If so, call or email the corporate office and ask someone there about the company's blog and archive of past publications.

In addition, you might go online to the company's websites and see if there is any information about a blog there as well. And, if all else fails, try Google. Better yet, if there are any industry associations, call or email them and ask if any company or industry blogs are presently active.

What did you learn from this exercise?

Bibliography

Baer, J. (2018). *The 13 Critical Podcast Statistics of 2018.* Convinceandconconvert.com

Bejou, D., Keiningham, T.L., & Aksoy, L. editors (2006). *Customer Lifetime Analysis: Reshaping the Way We Manage to Maximize Profits. (Vol 5, NO 2)* Journal of Relationship Marketing Vol 5, No. 2.

The Benefits of Postage Meters vs. Stamps & Online Postage. Fpusa.com.

Bigfoot Digital. *Do You Follow the 4-1-1 Social Media Rule?* Bigfootdigital.co.uk.

Business.com (2019). *AgoraPulse Review.* Business.com.

Business.com (2018), *Best Broker List Services* in 2018. Business.com.

The Best in Targeted Direct Mail. (2018). Dbmmailandcreative.com.

Bly, R. W. *The 12 Most Common Direct Mail Mistakes …And How to Avoid Them.* Marketingtoday.com.

Brodie I. (2017). *Email Persuasion*, Rainmaker Publishing.

Burnett, L. (October 4, 1960), Speech presented to the Chicago Copywriter's Club.

Businessdictionary.com.

CDC.Gov (2014), *Deaths in the US.* Centerfordiseasecontrol.gov.

Cerny, M. (2015). *Simple Analytics to Turn Your Data into a Goldmine.* Mirekcerny.com.

Chaffey, D. D. (2018). Digital Marketing Planning Template. Smartinsights.com.

Collinsdictionary.com.

Connor, T. (2003). *Soft Sell: The New Art of Selling.* Naperville: Source Books, Inc.

Coupon Facts (2017). Yellowdogpublishing.com.

Data & Mailing Lists. Compu-mail.com.

Databases vs. Spreadsheets, 365 Data Science, Sept. 14, 2018. 365Datascience.com.

Data & Marketing Association (2017) *Statistical Fact Book.*

David Bejou, P., Timothy L. Keiningham, M. B. A., & Lerzan (Eds.). (2006). *Customer Lifetime Value: Reshaping the Way We Manage to Maximize Profits.* New York: Routledge, Taylor & Francis Group.

Decile Analysis. Totalcustomeranalytics.com.

DesJardins, J. (Jan 27, 2016). *Calculating the Lifetime Value of a Customer.* Visualcapitalist.com.

Determann, J. (Feb. 10, 2015). *Understanding Net Present Value vs. Lifetime Value,* The Weinstein Organization. Twochicago.com.

De Veirmann, M. (2015). *Facts Versus Feelings? The Effectiveness of Hard Sell versus Soft Sell Appeals in Online Advertising*, University of Gent. Biblio.ugent.be.

Digital Marketing Plan. OneNetInc.com

Dillman, D. A. (1978). *Mail and Telephone Surveys*. New York: John Wiley & Sons.

Direct Mail Advertising Will Work for You: It Has A Low Cost and High ROI. Mspark.com.

Direct Mail ROI Calculator. Printngforless.com.

Direct Mail VS. Email: Who is King? (2015). Socialmediaweekd.org.

Direct Marketing Versus Database Marketing. (2008) Retailmarketingblog.com.

Dolnicar, S., Grun, B., & Leisch, F. (2018). *Market Segmentation Analysis*. Singapore: Springer Open Access Books.

Email Statistics Report, 2018-2022. The Radicati Group, Inc. Radicati.com.

Finn, A. (2017). *Email Marketing Device & Demographic Statistics*. Wordstream.com

Finn, A. (2018). *35 Face-Melting Email Marketing Stats for 2018*. Wordstream.com

Forer, L. (2017). *Cost Per Acquisition: Direct Mail Vs. Email Infographic*. Marketingprofts.com.

Frost, A. (2018). *The Ultimate Guide to Direct Mail*. Blog.hubspot.com.

Gould, S. (2017). *Five Ways to Spice Up Your Direct Mail Marketing in 2017*. Forbes.com.

Greenfader, B. Which Has Better ROI: Direct Mail or Social Media. Enthusem.com/blog.

Grigsby, M. (2018). *Marketing Analytics*. New York: Kogan Page Ltd.

Grumbine, J. (2018). *How Many People Move Each Year in the United States?* Quora.com.

Hatch, D., & Jackson, D. (1997). *2239 Tested Secrets for Direct Marketing Success*. Chicago: NTC Business Books.

History of Bankers Trust New York Corporation, Fundinguniverse.com.

How to Choose the Best Blogging Platform in 2018 (Compared). Wpbefinner.com

How to Start A Successful Blog. Hubspot.com.

Hughes, A. (2010). *Quick Profit with RFM Analysis*. Databasemarketinginstitute.com.

Jami, C. (2011). *Salome: In Every Inch in Every Mile*. Goodreads, Poem #65.

Keller, K. (April 7, 2017). *CMS Battle for Beginners, Wordpress vs. Joomla vs. Drupal*, Entrepreneur.com.

Kennedy, D.S. (2013). *The Guide to No B.S. Direct Marketing*, Second Edition, Entrepreneur Press.

Kopecky, J. (2017). *An Investigation into the ROI of Direct Mail vs. Email Marketing*. Hubspot.com/blog.

Laracuente, E. (2016). *Statistics That Prove Why Direct Mail Is Still King*. Resourcesolutions.com.

Larsson, T. (2016). *Ecommerce Evolved*. Buildgrowscale.com.

Larsson, T. (2010). *The 6 Figure Sales Funnel.* DigitalLowDown.

Lewin, K. (1952). Field Theory in Social Science: Selected Theoretical Papers, London: Tavistock.

Malthouse, E.C. (2013). Segmentation and Lifetime Value Models Using SAS, Cary, NC: SAS Institute, Inc.

R. Martharoo (2/12/2018), *Infusionsoft vs. Clickfunnels: Best for Your Business?* YouTube.

MelissaDirect.com, MCOA & pCOS Change of Address, Melissadirect.com.

McManus, L., & Nerney, A. (2018). How to Start A Blog, Createandgo.com.

Medhora, N. (2016). *What is Direct Mail Marketing?* Kopywritingkourse.com.

Mening, R (2019). *How to Create a Website,* Websitesetup.org.

Merriam-Webster Dictionary, Merriam-Webster.com.

Montanez, E. (2014). *Direct Mail Is Not Dead.* Corona, CA: Anoroc Publishing.

Moreau, E. (2018). *The 10 Best Social Media Management Applications.* Livewire.com.

Pack, S. (June 9, 2017). *What is the 4-1-1 Rule: Social Media Strategies for Successful Content Planning*, Marketing Matters. Skywestmedia.com.

Pitney-Bowes (2018). Changes Ahead for USPS Move Update Standard: What Mailers Need to Know, Pitneybowes.com.

Pulcinella, S. (2017). *Why Direct Mail Marketing Is Far from Dead.* August 30, 2017. Forbes.com.

Privy Academy (2017). *Why Building An Email List Matters?* *Privy.com*

Radicati Group, *Email Statistics Report*, 2018-2022, Radicati.com.

RFM Analysis for Successful Customer Segmentation, (2018) Putler.com

Rignvee, S. *How to Analyze Your A/B Test Results with Google Analytics.* Conversionxl.com.

Rust, R.T., Zeithaml, V., & Lemon, K.N. (2001). Driving Customer Equity: *How Customer Lifetime Value is Reshaping Corporate Strategy*, New York: The Free Press.

Sales Prospecting on Quora: 8 Easy Steps to Get Started. Blog.hubspot.com.

Saunders, A. (2018). *7 Powerful Sales Rose-Plays to Train Your Team,* Userlike.com.

Schember, J. (May 1, 2003). *When is NCOA Not Enough?* Target Marketing Magazine, Targetmarketingmag.com.

Simpson, C., & Kennedy, D. S. (2014). *The Direct Mail Solution.* Entrepreneur Press.

Smith, B. (2018). *7 Direct Response Marketing Techniques to Drive Action NOW. Wordstream.com.*

Social Media Advertising; Measure the ROI of Your Social Media Campaign; Create A Winning Social Media Strategy. Marketo.com.

Sonberg, J. (2017). *How to Build A Strong A/B Testing Plan That Gets Results.* Conversionxl.com

Statista.com. (2017). Estimated US Media Spending. Statista.com.

Statista.com. (2018), *Social Media Usage.* Statista.com.

Tedesco, T. J., Boone, K., Woods, T., & Leonard, J. (2002). *Direct Mail Pal: A Direct Mail Production Handbook.* PIA/GATF Press.

30 Direct Mail Statistics for 2017. Compu-mail.com.

U. S. Postal Service (2017), *Guide to Move Update.* Usps.com.

Visa Audiences: Find new, Lapsed, and Loyal Customers Across Mobile, Social, Display and Addressable TV and Video Channels. Visa.dk.

Wainwright, C. (2015). *Why Blog? The Benefits of Business Blogging.* Blog.hubspot.com

Webb, A. (2015). *How to Measure Social Media ROI.* ConversionXL.com

What is a Good Direct Mail Response Rate? Mccarthyandking.com.

White, C. S. (2017). *Email Marketing Rules: Checklists, Frameworks, and 150 Best Practices for Business Success.* Linkedin.com/ln/chadwhite.

Wilcox, R.T. (2003). *A Practical Guide to Conjoint Analysis.* Charlottesville, VA: Darden Business Publishing.

Williams, J. (Sept. 14, 2016). *Social Media: Marketing Strategies for Rapid Growth Using: Facebook, Twitter, Instagram, LinkedIn, Pinterest, and YouTube.* Published by John Williams.

INDEX

L

Letters, 20, 39-47, 50-66, *See*
    Templates, Junk Mail
Lists, 27, 28, 54, 58, 107, 118-119,
    See Email

M

Media spending, 14-15
Multichannel marketing, 121, 135-
    156, See Omnichannel marketing,
    Direct mail marketing, Email,
    Social Media, Blogging

N

Net Present Value (NPV), 128, 129
Nixies, 109, 111, *See* Data hygiene

O

Omnichannel marketing, 135-156.

P

Palletization, 117-118
Platforms
    Blogging
        Drupal, 154
        Joomla, 154
        Wordpress, 153-154
    Email
        Active Campaign, 151
        ClickFunnel, 150
        Constant Contact, 149
        Infusionsoft, 149-150
    Social Media
        AgoraPulse, 143
        Alliance Sweepstakes, 141-142

Hashtag Expert for IG, 141
Hootsuite, 138-139, 146-147
Tailor Social, 144
Thryv, 140
TweetDeck, 141
Podcasts, 152
Power words, 31, 40–41
Preheader texts, 149-150

Q

Q&A Format, 71
QR Barcodes, 19, 117

R

Response rates, 15, 18, 26, 28, 96,
    See RFM; Barcodes; Data
    hygiene; Email; Junk mail
RFM, 95–99
Rule 4-1-1, 144–146
Rule 70-20-10, 146

S

Social Media, 26, 27, 136-146, *See*
    Platforms
Stimulus-response, 23

T

Tagline, 90, 92, 93
Telemarketing, 72–74
Templates, 54
Tracking delivery, 115-116
Tri-fold brochure, 67-69

U

Unique Selling Proposition (USP), 88

Made in United States
North Haven, CT
04 October 2022

24981804R00095